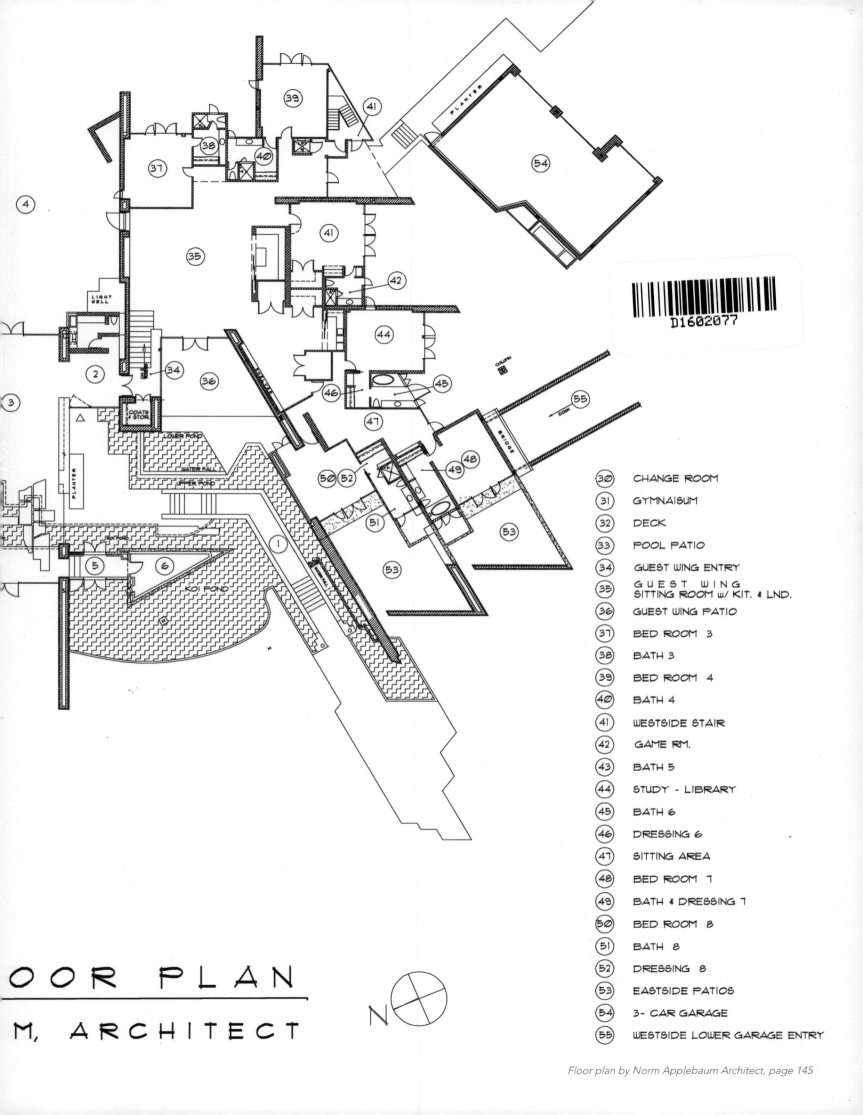

30	CHANGE ROOM
31	GYMNAISUM
32	DECK
33	POOL PATIO
34	GUEST WING ENTRY
35	GUEST WING SITTING ROOM w/ KIT. & LND.
36	GUEST WING PATIO
37	BED ROOM 3
38	BATH 3
39	BED ROOM 4
40	BATH 4
41	WESTSIDE STAIR
42	GAME RM.
43	BATH 5
44	STUDY - LIBRARY
45	BATH 6
46	DRESSING 6
47	SITTING AREA
48	BED ROOM 7
49	BATH & DRESSING 7
50	BED ROOM 8
51	BATH 8
52	DRESSING 8
53	EASTSIDE PATIOS
54	3- CAR GARAGE
55	WESTSIDE LOWER GARAGE ENTRY

OOR PLAN

M, ARCHITECT

N

Floor plan by Norm Applebaum Architect, page 145

THE MODERN
RESIDENCE

LS3P Architects, page 325

Inspired Modern Homes Imagined and
Designed by the Nation's Leading Architects

Published by
Intermedia Publishing Services, Inc.
5815 Richwater Drive
Dallas, TX 75252
972-898-8915

Publisher: Brian G. Carabet
Regional Publisher: Marc Zurba
Regional Publisher: Rick Esposito
Managing Editor: Katrina Autem
Editor: Lindsey Wilson
Editor: Rachel Watkins
Art Director: Adam Carabet
Production Coordinator: Vicki Lindsey

Printed in Malaysia

Distributed by Independent Publishers Group
800.888.4741

PUBLISHER'S DATA

THE MODERN RESIDENCE

Library of Congress Control Number

ISBN 13: 978-0-57859138-4

First Printing 2020

10 9 8 7 6 5 4 3 2 1

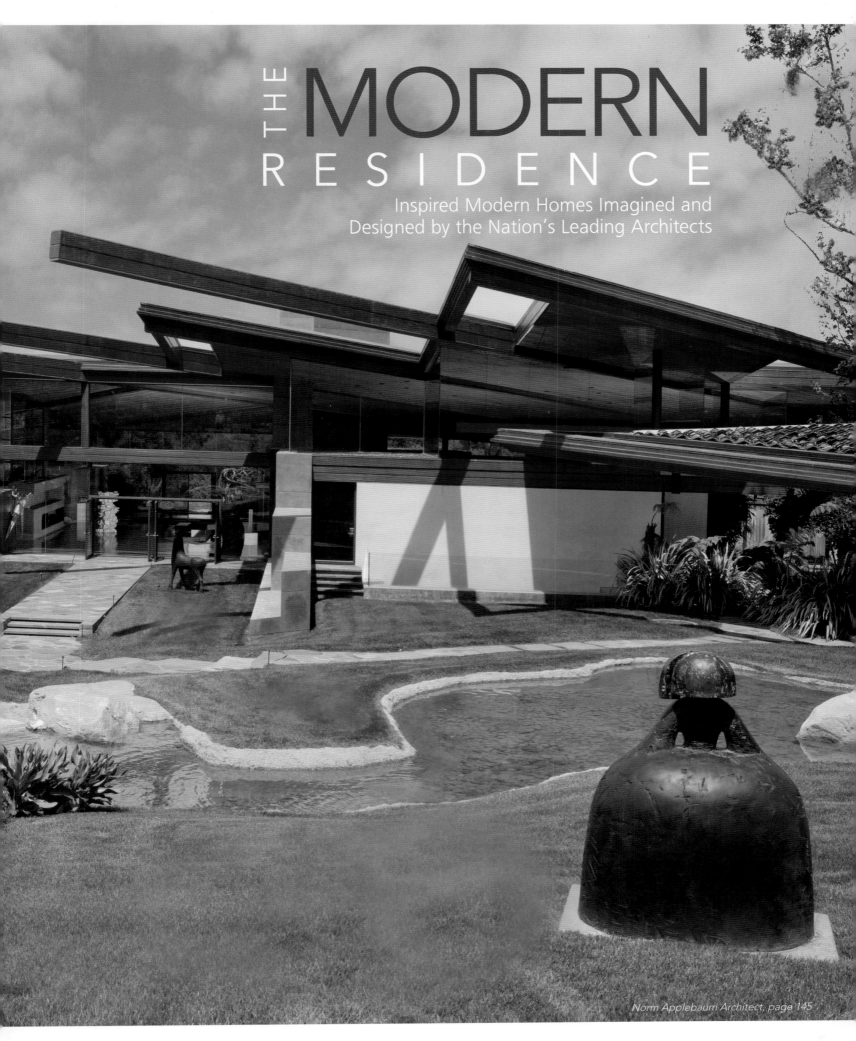

THE MODERN RESIDENCE

Inspired Modern Homes Imagined and
Designed by the Nation's Leading Architects

Norm Applebaum Architect, page 145

Murdough Design, page 455

INTRODUCTION

Every residence has its own personality, but when homes are created from masterful minds and skilled hands, there are a few things they have in common. The careful attention to proportion, light, and form can be seen in every space featured on the pages of *The Modern Residence*, regardless of the aesthetic or style. They have been thoughtfully designed to respond to the families who reside within, and seek to enhance the residents' overall quality and enjoyment of life. Modern architecture is not simply about shelter, it is art in the built form that seeks to improve lives—and the homes featured here do just that.

With dwellings that span the U.S. and Canada, you'll find homes from the southeast to the northeast, and from the west to the central United States. The geographic locations are diverse and each project presents its own set of benefits and challenges—topography, climate, and culture play key roles in shaping a home's design and function. Hammer Architects, for example, uses materials that make sense for the harsh conditions of the Atlantic Coast. One home sits atop a coastal bluff and is clad in western red cedar and mahogany that will change colors beautifully as it ages, and blends into the natural wooded landscape. Here, the home responds and adapts to its environment and is a direct reflection of its surroundings. In Aspen, Sinclair Building Architecture Design sources local materials whenever possible and works with the limited infrastructure available in mountainous terrain. The remote location is what makes the homes so appealing and also presents the biggest obstacle throughout the building phase. For Texas-based Malone Maxwell Borson Architects, the region's seasonal heavy rains can present specific challenges when designing a home. When the firm worked on a site that sat adjacent to a floodplain, the house had to be carefully integrated into the site's considerable natural grade. The slope was of the utmost importance and the design of the home benefited from strong elements that could withstand intense thunderstorms, with materials such as brick and cedar. These location-specific dwellings are distinct, stunning modern representations of their place and offer a sense of timelessness.

Behind these homes is a network of skilled professionals, and although architects are at the forefront of their projects, most of them will quickly admit that they would be nothing without their trusted teams. Interior designers, metalworkers, builders, woodworkers, and the support systems within the firms make it all possible. The architects and designers featured within these pages have not only built a reputation through their impressive work, but because they also bring the strongest, most trusted crews to every project. The homes featured on the pages of *The Modern Residence* are a testament to the talent of North American architectural teams.

Nahra Design Group, page 461

Morgante–Wilson Architects, page 273

ArchitecTor, page 17

Hays + Ewing Design Studio, page 315

"Architecture has been called the mother art for its all-encompassing nature combining sculpture, mathematics, engineering, anthropology and ecology. There couldn't be a greater challenge than creating meaningful, beautiful, enduring structures that enrich the lives of those that dwell within them."
—Chris Hays, AIA
Hays + Ewing Design Studio

McInturff Architects, page 449

Maryann Thompson Architects, page 443

John Grable Architects, Inc, page 249

Angelini & Associates Architects, page 223

"We endeavor to advance modernism in our region. We discover through this process that clients garner an appreciation and desire the attributes of modern architecture."
—John Grable, FAIA

Smith and Moore Architects, page 339

"The environment around us inspires the design. It is amazing to see a lot of the structures built today that show little or no awareness of it at all. When designing a structure, we have the opportunity to take advantage of the elements of our region—natural light, breezes, and the views are just a few of the design aspects."

—Jonathan Moore, AIA

Smith and Moore Architects

42 ° North - Architecture + Design, page 197

Altus Architecture + Design, page 215

S Barzin Architect, page 469

11

Maria Ogrydziak Architecture, page 121

The Nation's Finest Modern Architects

WESTERN US

CENTRAL US

Demetriou Architects, page 55

Bruns Architecture, page 229

Table of Contents

SOUTHEASTERN US

NORTHEASTERN US

Richard Luke Architects, page 173

Maria Ogrydyziak Architecture, page 121

Donald Joseph Architects, page 67

Reid Smith Ar... ...age xxx

WESTERN US

BELOW & FACING PAGE: Carefully tailored to the clients wishes, this home is nearly 9,000 square feet and is an effortless blend of Old World charm with contemporary style and amenities. We created large glass walls topped with clerestory windows that retract into the walls, opening the main living space to the outdoors. Organic colors and rustic finishes connect the space with its desert surroundings.
Photograph below by Stephen Thompson Photography
Photograph facing page by Joe Cotitta, Epic Photography

ArchitecTor

Tor Stuart, principal architect and founder of ArchitecTor, embraces the colors, textures, and views of the natural environment by integrating abundant indoor-outdoor living spaces and effectively creating an environment that lives much larger than the contained floor area. Tor creates homes in harmony with nature, where the goal is for the architecture to take on a chameleon-like quality, even disappearing into the landscape from certain angles. He uses elements such as cantilevers, long spans, and retracting window walls to integrate unique, contemporary engineering into homes.

For more than 25 years, Tor Stuart's body of work has balanced delicate detail and bold complexities inspired by the beauty of the land. Working in styles from contemporary to traditional, from modern to pueblo, Tor strives to design homes that form a union with their site, where visual delights await around every corner. Inspired by the natural textures and colors of the Sonoran Desert, he creates homes that fit harmoniously with the land. Growing up in Norway, Tor was fascinated by ancient Norwegian vegetative roof systems. That fascination evolved into a powerful belief in the importance of green architecture and sustainable design. ArchitecTor projects increasingly rely on sustainable features such as net-zero energy consumption and taking advantage of the natural light.

BELOW & FACING PAGE: Walls of light-colored Canyon Castle stone, dark-stained wood ceiling beams, and vintage barnwood shelves offer a rustic mountain feel, while the six-foot-tall by five-foot-wide fireplace with a chevron-patterned firebox brings a touch of the French countryside indoors. Opposite the comfortable seating area is a sizeable kitchen. We made a vast curved breakfast counter, flanked by a matching wooden appliance tower, which delineates the space while keeping it open to the views. Symmetrical at its center, the overhanging framework and negative-edge pool forms a matrix focal point of this hillside hideaway. Dramatic framework underlines my trademark use of symmetry to draw the eye through the house and out to the stunning views of the valley beyond. A linear see-through fireplace frames the views of the city and mountain peaks on the horizon. A sunken seating area separates the fireplace and the pool.
Photographs by Stephen Thompson Photography

Lot 231 The Saguaro Forest, Desert Mountain

Lot 231 The Saguaro Forest, Desert Mountain

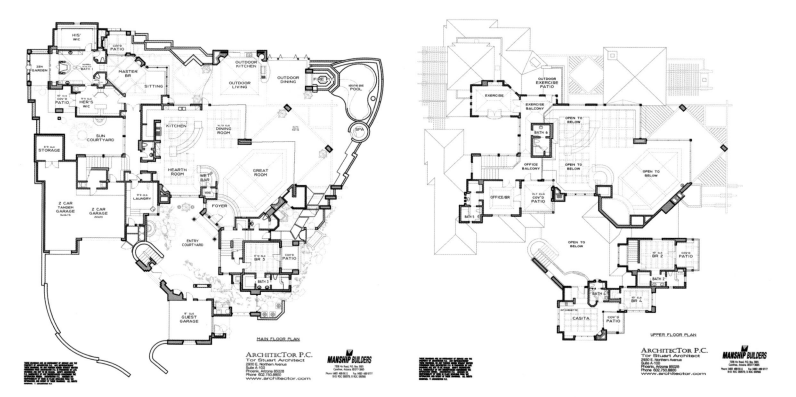

"The spectacular desert valley vistas inspired the use of floor-to-ceiling glass walls that open up to expansive panorama views and frame the beautiful scenery beyond."
—Tor Stuart

BELOW TOP & BOTTOM: Careful symmetry and floor-to-ceiling glass enhances the entrance to this dramatic hillside retreat. Nestled in its own private and gated 10-acre hidden canyon, this spectacular home offers serenity and tranquility with million-dollar views of the valley beyond. A modern-organic palette of custom stonework blends the exteriors with the unspoiled desert surroundings.
Photographs by Stephen Thompson

"The landscape design is an extension of your living area and an essential part of the overall design of your home. From your front entry to your backyard pool, creating a year-round retreat is one of our favorite aspects of the final design. The purpose of a successful landscape design is to integrate the architecture with the natural surroundings, creating a unity between your home and nature."
—Tor Stuart

BELOW TOP: The homeowners bought this property for its spectacular views and private setting. A custom-designed, negative-end lap pool reflects the rosy-colored setting desert sun. Clever and careful design makes the rest of the world disappear once you walk through the front door.

BELOW BOTTOM: Floor-to-ceiling glass doors disappear and retract into thick, stone-covered walls making for an expansive backyard retreat. We used the same grey stone flooring throughout to create a smooth transition between indoor-outdoor living spaces.
Photographs by Stephen Thompson

"Above all, I believe that a house can and should be a work of art you can live in—an enduring expression of each client's aesthetic. It's all about creating a successful design relationship where we fuse their vision with our creativity."
—Tor Stuart

FACING PAGE TOP: A custom 15-foot rainfall water feature that plunges into the 80-foot (25 meter) lap pool creates a unique experience in this one-of-a-kind backyard oasis.

FACING PAGE BOTTOM: A large fireplace covered with black-stone tile anchors the focal point in the great room. Sleek and modern furnishings complement the architecture and are an important aspect of the overall design.

TOP: We created clean lines to define the kitchen and bar with dark-wood custom cabinetry. Complemented by marble counters and backsplash, this contemporary kitchen is a chef's dream. Custom floor-to-ceiling wine shelves separate the bar from the front entrance.
Photographs by Stephen Thompson

CENTER & BOTTOM: The master bedroom fireplace is clad in a custom-stacked stone inspired by the natural environment. We incorporated the amazing colors of the surrounding desert, reflected in this peaceful retreat overlooking the desert and valley views beyond.
Photograph by Tony Hernandez

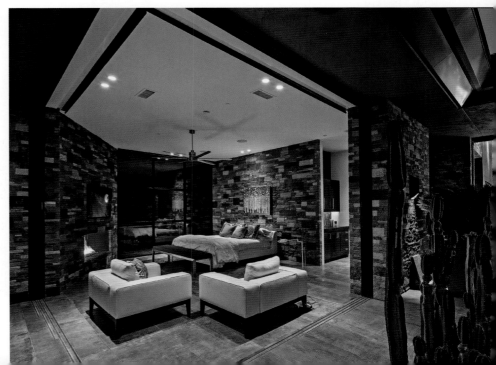

BELOW: The Cherry Hills residence is nestled into a wide two-acre triangular lot, which created the potential to upgrade its curb-side appeal. The homeowner desired to leave the original footprint of the existing Cape Cod-style home undisturbed as an effort of sustainability.

FACING PAGE: Many new, larger windows were strategically located to allow more light throughout the home. The thin, dark aluminum frames give way to spacious openings, bringing a welcomed transparency to the exterior.
Photographs by Ed LaCasse

Architectural Workshop

Architectural Workshop (AW) was conceived in 1999 by founder Mark Bowers. The Denver-based firm was created from the desire to provide a greater level of creativity, innovation, and excellence in architecture. AW approaches design with a team mentality, and the firm's experience shows that the best project solutions come from a qualified group of design professionals who have a history of problem solving and creative solutions.

Architectural Workshop is committed to taking ordinary projects and making them extraordinary. The design approach of every project incorporates four design criteria: creativity, innovation, sustainability, and uniqueness—all are equally important. Creativity is the ability to see beyond the obvious, to imagine a design that allows a project to go beyond its constraints and achieve the highest level of architecture possible. Innovation takes the available resources and uses experience, knowledge, and talent to build a composition where the total is greater than the sum of its parts. Sustainable design seeks out the most practical balance between the natural and the built environment through a careful combination of the site amenities, construction methods, and building materials. Uniqueness means every project, like every living object, should be created to be unique to its location, its function, and to the purpose for which it is intended.

"Diversity and a passion for excellence fuel my work."
—Brett Linscott

LEFT: The owners were looking for a design strategy that respected the long-standing neighborhood without restricting new ideas and modern living. Raising the second floor and increasing transparency on the main level was paramount in achieving this vision. The sensible result combined a new urban chic genre with an Old-World industrial flair. We used heavy, stacked timber stairs with leather tread inlays. The railing system is comprised of delicate metal spindles, transparent enough not to impede the dramatic view into the living space.

FACING PAGE TOP & BOTTOM: Raw, brushed metal finishes are fashioned throughout the interior with glimpses of concrete surfaces from the open kitchen. Two islands were positioned 90 degrees from the back wall to frame the food preparation functionality desired by the food-loving clients. This exposed layout interfaces not only the dining room, but also the family room and breakfast nook, resulting in a full 180-degree exposure to its surroundings.

Photographs by Emily Minton Redfield

BELOW: To achieve their vision, the design team focused on balancing the old country club estate aesthetic with a move toward a refined, rural vernacular. This is evident in the living room. Two huge 15-foot sliding openings flow into a covered patio beyond which subtly brings the outside in.

FACING PAGE: Board and batten siding provide warmth and nostalgia. Reclaimed horizontal boards were utilized sparingly to offer not only contrast, but a historical nod to the rural surroundings.
Photographs by Emily Minton Redfield

"I approach every project with creativity, enthusiasm, and a commitment to quality."
—Joe Marshall

BELOW: For the Cornell residence, we used soft hues for surfaces and natural light throughout the home—all deftly complemented by mid-century-appropriate style lines. The result is a crisp, cohesive aesthetic. The material palette has a warm, rich foundation of woods, used on floors, ceilings, cabinetry, and millwork in the main living space.
Photographs by Ed LaCasse

BELOW TOP & BOTTOM: Seeking to enrich lives and the living experience, our primary goal was to preserve and reimagine a 1950s home as a continuum of architectural history and engineering science. Our design-build team acquired a property in Arapahoe Acres, a mid-century development consisting of 124 similarly designed homes originally conceived as contemporary, affordable, family-centric housing. Placing daily, family interaction at the center of decision-making, the redesign envisioned a prototypical home that was classically stylish in disposition and forward-thinking in environmental embrace. The home achieved a sustainable goal of net-zero living through the incorporation of geothermal and photovoltaic energy generation systems. Combined with smart home features, the house can respond to changing conditions and owner desires to be more efficient and provide a higher level of comfort.
Photographs by Ed LaCasse

"My passion is to create architecture that incorporates the art of form, function, and beauty that goes beyond the utilitarian to touch the emotions."
—Mark Bowers

BELOW: The design begins with the intention of creating a heart of the home, an epicenter from which all activity and interaction spirals outward into the yard flowing through other smaller, private spaces. Eliminating the overbearing sense of compartmentalization was a high priority and opening the home's potential meant creating a large airy volume of central living space by extending the kitchen up and out and including floor-to-ceiling windows.

FACING PAGE: The homeowner has said that the simplicity and openness of the design along with the clean views through the home allow for their full use of the interior and exterior features as a family. This renovation and addition not only took the existing 850 square feet to a more livable 2,025-square-foot home, but also produced a sustainable home that holds continual interaction as a core value of healthy family living.
Photographs by Ed LaCasse

BELOW & FACING PAGE: The homeowners relocated from Marin County to Manhattan's Upper East Side, with the goal of adding the warm, gentle, and fun spirit of California to their newly acquired 1,700-square-foot apartment. Originally the home felt confining, narrow, and dark, but I raised parts of the ceiling in sweeping shapes and turned walls into wide columns that hid pipes and structural elements.
Photographs by Charles Callister, Jr.

Architecture Studio

It's not unusual for children to dream about what they want to be when they grow up, but few actually make it a reality. Since the age of nine, however, Elida Doldan-Schujman has known she would be an architect. Growing up the daughter of a playwright in Buenos Aires, Argentina, she spent her formative years watching set designers—many of whom were also architects— construct fantastic façades onstage. After studying architecture at Arizona State University, Doldan-Schujman opened her own firm in 1983 and set about giving her clients their own personal stage sets upon which their lives could play out.

An avid traveler, Doldan-Schujman draws inspiration from far-flung corners of the world and incorporates diverse cultural ideas into her designs. Environmental impact is at all times top of mind, as she strives to responsibly construct buildings that are energy efficient and produce as little waste as possible while supporting her clients' wishes and vision. A strong connection to nature and the outdoors is always a priority, while she embraces the challenges that come with urban, historic, and conservatively sized projects, as well.

BELOW: I carved out new walls around existing structural steel frames, fitting in display niches while providing transparency from space to space and giving the illusion of larger rooms. The color scheme and the materials used represent memories of California: light-colored walls, blond-wood bamboo floors, birds-eye and rotary maple cabinets and paneling, recycled-content countertops, paper stone surfaces, and energy efficient touches throughout. While New York did not require compliance to title 24 or to a Green Residential Code, we still built it as we would in California.

FACING PAGE TOP: I designed the built-in furniture as well as the area carpets. With opposing curves to the ceiling, the carpets give movement to an otherwise static space. I tried to trick the eye into feeling the rooms are wider and taller than they are, and to allow the perimeter natural light to travel into the interior spaces through glass doors and clerestory windows. An outdoor space to barbecue and relax was a must, and this apartment did have a terrace with an outstanding view of the city. The overall result of the apartment design is a warm and relaxing refuge from the high-energy New York City lifestyle.
Photographs by Charles Callister, Jr.

BELOW & FACING PAGE: My clients imagined a ring-shaped house with a central courtyard overlooking the hills and valleys beyond their property in Silicon Valley, California. At the entry foyer, mirrors triplicate the floor's marble pattern, creating a full-circle design while also reflecting the views of the adjacent hillside. Wood paneling at doorways denotes the transition from space to space, and scalloped vaulted ceilings emphasize the ring effect of the design.
Photographs by Charles Callister, Jr.

BELOW & FACING PAGE: This soft mountain contemporary-style home sits on a corner lot in Aspen's coveted West End, thus creating a visually dynamic exterior from all aspects. Capturing sunlight throughout the day, this home is enjoyable during every Colorado season. The use of approachable elements, such as stone, wood, and metal, celebrates the historic character of the neighborhood while expressing its own unique style.
Photographs by Gibeon Photography

Brewster McLeod Architects

This award-winning boutique architecture firm, based in Aspen Colorado, specializes in luxury residential architecture from San Francisco to Washington D.C., and internationally. Since the firm's inception, Jamie L. Brewster McLeod, has strived to provide exceptional design that truly brings out a sense of place.

Jamie's focus is creating architecture as living art forms designed perfectly within their natural environments. The result is architecture set naturally within the landscape creating the setting for each custom creation.

The goal of each design is to ensure all elements of the homeowners' desires are expressed with stylistic insight and thoughtful design, thus creating a relationship with her clients that transforms their dreams into reality.

As an all-inclusive custom firm, Brewster McLeod Architects is there from the initial ideas throughout the construction and final finishing touches that each home deserves.

BELOW TOP: Clean, artistic stairs help celebrate the circulation space in the center of the home, creating a central art piece viewed on all three levels.

BELOW BOTTOM LEFT: Since the homeowners are oenophiles as well as winemakers, we created a custom wine room as a focal point to the lower floor living area.

BELOW BOTTOM RIGHT: An open floor plan throughout the main floor creates the ideal entertaining space. The inlay-wood ceiling provides a rustic touch that balances the modern elements of the state-of-the-art kitchen, fit for a chef.

FACING PAGE: High ceilings in the living room help filter natural light into the open main floor living spaces while highlighting the modern stone fireplace feature.
Photographs by Gibeon Photography

BELOW & FACING PAGE: Nicknamed "the flying wing" by original architect Harry Gesner, this house built for a lumber magnate became a showcase for wood, including a structural system of wood poles. After being literally saved from the wrecking ball, we set out to liberate the home from its heavy walls and have every room open up to its spectacular 270-degree views.
Photographs by Adrian Van Anz

Dean Larkin Design

Dean Larkin, AIA has been described as the quintessential Los Angeles architect. His contemporary style and affinity for luxurious indoor-outdoor living have earned him a reputation as the problem-solver of typically difficult Southern California sites—think homes built into a hillside, or unusually shaped lots that require extra ingenuity and planning. Having grown up in L.A. and founded his practice here in 1999, Dean is especially familiar with the area's stringent regulations. Where others see problems, he sees potential.

As a result, his clients seek him out to turn naturally beautiful but challenging sites into spectacular homes that evoke the unique climate, attitude, and lifestyle of Southern California. Dean eschews the simple geometrical uniformity of modern architecture and instead strives for a multi-layered complexity that is both effortless and elegant. His background in traditional architecture—which required historical accuracy and getting every detail precisely right—gives him an edge over his peers and affects his overall approach.

Since graduating from the University of Southern California's respected School of Architecture, Dean had the honor of being the first employee of Richard Landry, founder of Landry Design Group. Working there allowed him to design many high-end residential and luxury destination projects all over the world. While there, *Architectural Digest* featured many of the homes prepared under his careful preparation, including the Hunts Point residence of Kenny G.

BELOW & FACING PAGE: We gutted the original structure, abandoned most of the original plan, increased the square footage by moving the garage to a separate structure, and completely redesigned the house to take advantage of a spectacular site, which can see all the way to the beach on a clear day. Exterior walls were expanded under the existing roof line and given a whole new level of transparency to its surrounding views on both levels. In addition, we tripled the size of the yard with new retaining walls and a spectacular curved pool placed on axis with the house to emphasize the views. The reimagined house celebrates the site and our 21st century lifestyle; as a result, it will be an architectural beacon for generations to come.
Photographs by Adrian Van Anz

BELOW & FACING PAGE: Originally, this home had only a narrow window of a view so we turned the whole house perpendicular to take advantage of it. Stone walls help with privacy—as does being on a corner lot—but, within the home, all the exterior walls have the ability to disappear completely, truly opening the residence up to the outdoors. The master bedroom and living room, for example, open directly to the back courtyard.
Photographs by Adrian Van Anz

"Great architecture does more than just work; it transcends itself, its occupants, and its environment."
—Dean Larkin

BELOW: One of our first forays into a high-rise design was this Century City residence, and the real challenge was to take our aesthetic and put it into a high-density home. Originally, the condo was large but dated, and the great view—which stretches all the way to Malibu and Santa Monica— was obscured. Why would you want to face any other way than the window?

FACING PAGE: The condo had a second floor that could only be accessed by a tiny spiral staircase, and that just wouldn't do. We installed a grand staircase and replaced all the doors and windows, getting to entirely reshape the rooms as a result.
Photographs by Adrian Van Anz

"When we get a hold of a project, we make sure to shake all the potential out of it."
—Dean Larkin

BELOW: Located in the famous "bird streets," where several celebrities live, this home had to be jaw-dropping. We were able to take over the design when it was just a foundation, so we enlarged it to nearly 6,000 square feet and took full advantage of the site's jetliner views. Key to the project is the dramatic placement of the swimming pool: You can literally step from the living area, through a sliding wall of glass, and into the dramatic knife-edge pool. Lit with color-changing LEDs, the pool becomes a kinetic work of art.

FACING PAGE: We tried to complement the client's Hollywood-hipster lifestyle. The design fully integrates the rear yard into the home's main level. The master suite, located on the main level, has a covered seating area that extends the sleeping area to the outside by the extensive use of wood ceilings and walls, enclosed only by draperies.
Photographs by Adrian Van Anz

BELOW & FACING PAGE: In response to a tight lot and the needs of an active family with young children, the arrangement of spaces provides definition of function without enclosure. Spaces borrow from each other, both horizontally and vertically. Photographs by John Granen

Demetriou Architects

Principal Vassos Demetriou began his career designing and building sets for plays during high school in his native Cyprus. He earned his architectural degree with graduate studies in cinematography from the University of Oregon, and after first practicing architecture in Europe, established the firm in the Seattle area in 1978. Michelle Demetriou Cozza grew up around the business, enjoying drawing, painting, and all things creative. Wanting to go into a field that would allow her to both be creative and contribute something meaningful, she also earned her degree in architecture at the University of Oregon, and specializes in interior architecture and design. Together, Vassos and Michelle manage Demetriou Architects, a full-service design firm specializing in custom residential architecture and interior architecture and design.

The firm was among the first to introduce international-style architecture to the Seattle/Eastside area. The clean lines, open interior spaces, and use of large expanses of glass with steel structures were natural complements to the Northwest's trees, water, and quality of light, and maximized the indoor-outdoor connection in a way new to the region. Though the firm's projects span a wide range of styles and locations, these tenets of the international style continue to embody their design vision.

BELOW & FACING PAGE: One of the hallmarks of Demetriou Architects' work is bringing together spaces within the house, as well as providing connection with the outdoors. Double-height glazing and a covered outdoor patio connect the indoor and outdoor living spaces with views of the lake.
Photographs by John Granen

*"Good architecture can
exist in any style."*
—Vassos M. Demetriou

"We approach every project with an open mind, free of stylistic preconceptions."
—Vassos M. Demetriou

BELOW & FACING PAGE: The form of this custom home, with its south setback set along a busy street, maximizes privacy from the street while bringing light into the house. Floor-to-ceiling glazing takes advantage of the water views towards the west. The open floor plan affords all spaces light and views. A vertical-grain cedar plank ceiling extends to the exterior, strengthening the indoor-outdoor connection. The entry courtyard emphasizes this connection with floor-to-ceiling glazing and stone sculptures in a shallow pool that can be enjoyed from inside the home.
Photographs by Mike Seidl

BELOW & FACING PAGE TOP: The house is stepped to respond to the steeply sloping lot. Full-height glazing and outdoor rooms at each level take full advantage of the 180-degree view of the lake, and provide indoor/outdoor connection.
Photographs by Michael Walmsley

FACING PAGE CENTER & BOTTOM: The client wanted a home equipped for professional-level cooking and entertaining large groups that was both warm and inviting—and impressive. Familiar materials were used in innovative ways: In the kitchen, art glass backsplash panels slide to reveal a full-width appliance garage, backlit resin panels in the ceiling provide an all-over glow, and a masonry modern Rumford fireplace serves as a pizza oven and indoor roasting spit. Wood panels at the dining and living room ceilings help to define the spaces and provide texture, warmth, and visual interest to the ceiling plane. Opaque resin panels with fabric interlay in the custom doors provide texture and light while maintaining privacy.
Photographs by Andrew O'Neill

BELOW & FACING PAGE: The design of this San Juan island weekend retreat is guided by its waterfront, wooded site. Indoor-outdoor connections are emphasized with expanses of glass to the view, materials such as corten steel and concrete that are continuous from exterior to interior, and columns whose forms echo the shape of the trees. An important design directive was to deal with the site in an environmentally sensitive way. A grass-crete driveway and grass-paver patios blur and minimize hard surfaces on the site, and the thoughtful treatment of the shoreline is now used as an example by the local jurisdiction for developments at the water's edge.
Photographs by Michael Jensen

"The design should reflect the user's needs and lifestyle, expressed in an artful and memorable way."
—Vassos M. Demetriou

BELOW & FACING PAGE: This house on a wooded site is organized around an indoor pool. The glazed enclosure provides both a visual and spatial connection between the house and the outdoors; lift-and-slide doors between the house and pool and to the patio create a dynamic space that allows for expansion of the living areas, or bringing the outdoors in. Just off the pool, the curved Brazilian cherry staircase features parallel rails that appear to change when seen from various angles, becoming an artful form which sculpts and helps define space horizontally and vertically. *Photographs by Gregg Krogstad, Krogstad Photography*

BELOW & FACING PAGE: Situated in the scenic Sacramento suburb of Granite Bay, surrounded by valley and blue oaks, granite outcroppings, and abundant wildlife, this residence is chiseled into its natural environment. Perched on a ridgetop, it flows and tumbles down the site imitating nature as bold and modern sculpture, both geometric and organic.
Photographs by Kat Alves

Donald Joseph Inc.

Donald Joseph Inc. is as much about human behavior as it is about architecture. Led by Donald J. Fugina Jr., the full-service firm seeks to understand the homeowners before conceptualizing their house. This requires insight into the family's culture, preferences, lifestyle, and unique traits. He works through all facets before designing a home; it has to meet their needs on all levels. After more than 40 years in the industry, Donald knows that his goal for each project is to create distinct expression of the homeowners' lives—all done with a good dose of humility.

The firm specializes in custom residential architecture, but offers much more than that. Site selection, master planning, and view analysis are fundamental elements of the team's unique design approach. Custom remodeling, interior architecture, finish selections, and furnishings round out the comprehensive practice. Donald Joseph Inc. is based in the greater Sacramento region of northern California with projects in the western United States.

"It's about the people. I don't design houses for awards."

—Donald J. Fugina Jr.

TOP: The entry foyer ceiling is defined by a wood-veneer, cantilevered cube which floats from the front to back of the building. Strong shapes and planes are defined with organic materials—walnut, aluminum, oak—expressing timeless design.

LEFT: Look through the floating stairs and you weightlessly ascend over a reflecting pool which starts at the front of the residence, flows under the foyer to the main terrace, and finally cascades into the swimming pool at the rear terrace, all of which float above the massive granite outcropping.

FACING PAGE TOP: The kitchen, located in the middle of the residence, floats at the sink base which overlooks an intimate eating courtyard beyond, complete with daily grill and tree-lined terrace. The space is centered on a 15-foot clerestory light well with a suspended light fixture cluster. High-end laminate cabinetry and quartz countertops are accented with Ann Sacks mosaic tile backsplash. The butler pantry is tucked beyond.

FACING PAGE BOTTOM: A 14-foot-tall automatic sliding-glass room corner connects the main gathering room to the outside terrace. Sky, trees, and water complete the sensual experience of connected spaces. Strong forms and solid materials define the floors, walls, and ceiling. Floating copper panels, cut stone, and limestone embellish the fireplace.
Photographs by Kat Alves

BELOW: The open iconic architectural entry welcomes visitors. It presents a strong visual connection linking the circular drive and front porch arrival experience to the interior, and the expansive rear yard beyond—naturally drawing visitors into the home.

FACING PAGE: The house's new raised and folding roof line provides an added level of depth to the front façade. Various layers of glazing appear and descend like distant hills in the landscape, drawing interest towards the interior of the home. At the same time, from an internal experience, they engage treetop views of the surrounding yard and bring them into the home.
Photographs by Karen Mercier of KREATIF Photography

Form Environmental Research – (fer) studio

The best rooms provoke thought and encourage imagination; they both focus and transcend an experience; they connect to other places, other times, and other worlds while simultaneously being in the present. This is what (fer) studio calls Trans-relational Environments—and it defines their work. Their goal is to provide a home, an office, or even a city that is a structured solution to help their clients build the most creative life possible; to design the lives they only dreamed of.

Founded in 2002, (fer) studio offers innovative, contemporary architectural and urban design solutions that address specific challenges through uniquely iconic and individually tailored architecture. To do this, the team of talented design professionals believes that three basic conditions must be studied and applied: form, environment, and research. Indeed, those are the letters by which the acronym (fer) is derived.

For president and design principal Christopher Mercier, it's also about practicing his love of art on the much grander scale that is architecture. His artist's eye—he maintains a dual practice as a contemporary painter—is never far from any of his projects

He and his team find challenge, inspiration, and commitment in serving diverse clients and communities across the world, with project types that include everything from cultural institutions, to educational facilities, corporate offices, commercial and retail locations, restaurants and hotels, and single and multi-family residences. In addition, they provide urban design solutions for larger cultural, educational, and civic municipalities.

BELOW: The home's most easily recognizable Trans-relational Environment—an environment that blurs boundaries and intertwines one spatial experience with the next—is the space that encompasses the outdoor dining room and kitchen. This transitional experience seamlessly merges the interior and exterior, moving from kitchen, to dining room and living room, to the outside dining and kitchen area, to the pool and finally the yard beyond.

FACING PAGE TOP: To meet the client's intentions, we completely reinvented this property to modernize it and make it more in tune with a resort-inspired design.

FACING PAGE CENTER: The home already had a swimming pool, small horse barn, tennis court and small fruit tree orchard—all of which we kept, while reimagining various aspects of these elements. Through an extensive hardscape and landscape design approach, working with [Place] - Pakshong Landscape and Architecture Collaborative, we merged the entire exterior environment into a trans-relational experience that's directly tied to the architecture.

FACING PAGE BOTTOM: The architecture opens to the hardscape and landscape in so many locations that the house's interior and exterior environments blend into a single experience.

Photographs by Karen Mercier of KREATIF Photography

BELOW TOP: We spent a lot of time opening up and reimagining the relationships between the living room, dining room, and kitchen. The original home was highly separated and segmented with a circulation route that didn't support the type of direct connectivity between the spaces that client wanted.

BELOW BOTTOM LEFT: Natural light floods the sleek contemporary kitchen by Bulthaup, all framed by the upper clearstory windows and a direct visual connection from kitchen sink to the pool—something the client highly desired.

BELOW BOTTON RIGHT: In the living room and kitchen, we raised and folded the ceiling to develop areas of raised expanse and others of more enclosed privatization. We introduced clearstory views along the north, linking the house to the outside landscape and allowing the adjacent treetops to become visible from the inside—again linking the surrounding environment to the interior space.
Photographs by Karen Mercier of KREATIF Photography

BELOW TOP: When the living room doors are completely open and you walk from the kitchen to the barbeque area to the poolside fire pit—traveling from the interior, to a semi-covered space, to completely outside—you experience it as a single cohesive environment. That continuity is exactly what we wanted to evoke.

BELOW BOTTOM: Even in the master bathroom, continuity is achieved through the use of natural stones and neutral tones that connect this space to the rest of the house via similar colorways and materials.
Photographs by Karen Mercier of KREATIF Photography

"The opportunity latent in the act of architecture is in finding ways of building walls that act more like bridges than boundaries; it is to uncover and explore the unrealized connectivity between form and environment through intensive design research."
—Christopher Mercier

BELOW: This ultra-contemporary, open-concept custom residence redefines architectural ingenuity with its steel, stucco, and glass aesthetic. We designed the structure in the shape of a horseshoe, representing two arms embracing.

FACING PAGE: Steel-clad portal columns create an intimate setting within the center garden.
Photographs by Robert Reck
The team for both homes featured in this profile is: Architects: Hoopes + Associates, Craig Hoopes, Andrea Caraballo; Interiors: Paul Rau Interiors,
Paul Rau, Betsy Bauer: Landscape: Serquis & Associates, Solange Serquis, Israel Munoz; Contractor: Prull Custom Homes, Will Prull

Hoopes + Associates

When Craig Hoopes was nine, he was intrigued by the entire construction process and end results—fast forward to now, and he's still fascinated by it all. Since the time he founded Hoopes + Associates in 1992, the firm has become one of Santa Fe's top studios, specializing in the design of custom homes, performing and assembly spaces, sacred spaces, and other custom places for end-users.

Hoopes + Associates is deeply committed to community, pragmatic design, and enduring architecture, infusing their designs with a modernist aesthetic that relies on form and minimalism and that is, above all, timeless and classic. Blurring the line between the indoors and outdoors is also a hallmark of their work, especially given Santa Fe's environment and seasons that beckon interaction. Their houses invite residents into the landscape while providing a sense of enclosure and protection.

As a boutique firm, Hoopes + Associates has stayed small by design in order to have close relationships with their clients that allow them to better understand their needs and concerns. They believe that architecture is a collaborative process; it is not created by one person sitting in a room and dreaming. Rather, it is many people dreaming together—client, architect, interior designer, landscape designer, contractor, and artisans. And, together, there is no challenge that cannot be met.

BELOW: Leading to the front door, the stucco walls simultaneously blend into their natural surroundings while defining their place in the landscape through a geometric aesthetic. We juxtaposed the desert landscaping with a custom water feature.

FACING PAGE TOP: The home incorporates several unique exterior structural designs, including a sweeping steel curved roof floating over the main living portal and a butterfly steel roof soaring above the guest portal.

FACING PAGE BOTTOM: The indoor living space seamlessly flows to the generous outdoor living area—one of several—through 12-foot sliding glass doors, uniting the interior and exterior.
Photographs by Robert Reck

"Our houses invite you into the landscape while also providing a sense of enclosure, protection."
—Craig Hoopes

"Inspiration comes from our clients. As we learn how they want to live their lives, we learn how space works for them."
—Craig Hoopes

ABOVE: The master bathroom is just as sumptuous as the free-flowing master suite and delivers ultimate privacy, yet is still seamlessly connected to the landscape through continuous glass walls.

RIGHT: This custom indoor shower sleekly integrates into the bathroom design with no need for doors.

FACING PAGE TOP: Custom in every detail, the main great room is punctuated by a massive piece of abstract art above the steel-clad biofuel fireplace that automatically lifts to reveal an 85-inch TV. The walls of glass connect the space to its natural surroundings, capturing the beautiful Sangre and Jemez mountain views for miles.

FACING PAGE BOTTOM: Connected to the great room, the state-of-the-art kitchen features elegant brown Brazilian quartzite countertops, straight grain white oak veneer cabinetry, a massive 15-foot-long central island, double dishwashers, and his-and-her sinks.
Photographs by Robert Reck

BELOW: This home sits on the edge of the Galisteo Basin, and with its big views, we wanted to ensure that the structure stretched into the landscape to make it feel a part of its environs. We designed it around a courtyard to provide protection from the winds and to extend the outdoor living season.

FACING PAGE TOP: Everything in the kitchen was designed to be as streamlined as possible, so that meant no cabinet hardware with most of the storage space allocated to the long center island.

FACING PAGE CENTER: A unique, custom fireplace defines and visually divides the living and dining areas in the great room.

FACING PAGE BOTTOM: Pocketing sliding glass doors open the interior to the exterior, blurring the definition between inside and outside.
Photographs by Daniel Nadelbach Photography, LLC

BELOW: Just three meters above sea level, the Saratoga Beach House forms part of a protected coastline in the heart of the windswept Oyster River Basin of Vancouver Island. The geometric dwelling acts as two organically interconnected frames; one mineral and one wood, both of which float above a virtually undisturbed site located between one of the world's richest marine tidal ecosystems to the northeast and a wetland preserve to the southwest.

FACING PAGE: The home is strategically built within a grove of 350-year-old Douglas fir trees, thus sharing their shelter and maintaining this essential habitat for bald eagles and a host of other wildlife. Preserving these majestic trees and pristine coast heavily influenced every aspect of this house and landscape design that was engineered to halt coastal erosion while rebuilding the coastal riparian beach.
Photographs by Brad Laughton

INTERSTICE Architects

After years of working in separate disciplines, Andrew Dunbar and Zoee Astrachan founded INTERSTICE Architects in the spirit of "total design"—a seamless integration of structure, place, materials, and innovation. The multidisciplinary firm includes architects, landscape architects, urban designers, and visual artists who design public and private spaces of varying scales yet the team always focuses on the broadest possible interpretation of the designed realm. That is to say, they embrace every opportunity to push the boundaries.

As such, diversity is a hallmark of INTERSTICE's mission, as they explore ideas that cross scale and discipline. Aside from celebrating this multiplicity of form, one of the most compelling influences behind the firm's work is rooted in ecological aspirations, often challenging conventions of form and public space. From developing small, highly detailed "urban furniture" installations to re-envisioning acres of coastal frontage as a response to the challenges of rising sea levels and bayside habitat degradation, the team is highly attuned to innovative architectural and landscape solutions.

The firm's work is also often an experiential response to broader issues and opportunities, leading to urban transformation—from reversing the loss of bird and insect habitats, to using repurposed waste stream materials, protecting and enhancing ancient trees, and creating minimalist, eco-aware solutions for complicated programs.

BELOW TOP: The elevated, seasonally closable guest house is mineral in nature, poetically connecting it to the land. It is constructed of fiber-reinforced concrete siding and steel, and its translucent, thermo-plastic doors form a mysterious, ghost-like effect at night.
Photograph by Brad Laughton

BELOW BOTTOM: The main house, seen in the background, is clad in the same local Douglas fir that surrounds it, stained grey to match these sun-bleached driftwood logs that litter the coast.
Photograph by Andrew Dunbar, INTERSTICE Architects

"Through compelling geometry and tall open spaces that frame the ocean and forest, a home becomes a room without walls from which to enjoy the pristine and ever-evolving landscape."
—Andrew Dunbar

BELOW: The main house is a warm wood structure with two-bedroom suites that are set off from the double-height living area. Carefully planned piers support the house while avoiding the tree roots below, allowing water and air to reach the soil and root system. With this "transparent footprint," the structure's impact on the native ecology is minimized.
Photograph by Brad Laughton

BELOW TOP: Under the guest house, cars park in a porte cochere that's concealed by folding translucent panels and accessed by a native grass reinforced driveway that is designed to disappear.
Photograph by Andrew Dunbar, INTERSTICE Architects

BELOW CENTER: An ample outdoor deck extends the view and further connects the indoors to the outdoors, as interior finishes pass from kitchen wall to outdoor shower concealed within the wood "frame."
Photograph by Brad Laughton

BELOW: The homeowner is originally from Calgary, where the Plus 15 Network is one of the most extensive, enclosed pedestrian sidewalk systems in the world. Inspired by this elevated network, the glass corridor is designed to connect the main house to the guest house through the surrounding fir canopies. Views from this bridge also accommodate the beautiful trees and plant life that surround the house.
Photograph by Brad Laughton

FACING PAGE BOTTOM: The home is designed to not only aesthetically resonate with the environment—its cladding spreads to allow air and light into the outdoor shower stall—but also to be sustainable in every possible way. For example, all structures collect rainwater, which is redistributed to the tree roots through a complex inverted branching supply system beneath the elevated structure.
Photograph by Andrew Dunbar, INTERSTICE Architects

"Beauty is often found in distilling the complex."
—Andrew Dunbar

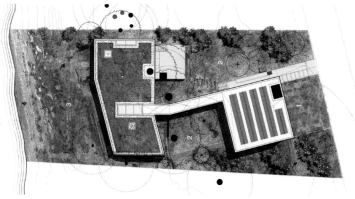

ABOVE, FACING PAGE TOP LEFT & RIGHT: As the owner wanted to build their home in sympathy with the ecological context to preserve the native habitat, we prioritized every single Douglas fir in the design and artfully allowed the age-old trees to "grow" through the home across the deck and patio spaces so they became a theatre of evergreen against the ocean's colorful canvas. The outdoor kitchen is concealed behind a vertically sliding panel in the wood frame on the garden side of the home, where a cascading wooden deck floats over and into the south court landscape.
Photographs by Brad Laughton and Andrew Dunbar, INTERSTICE Architects

CENTER AND BOTTOM: A bird's eye view shows the home's two interconnected buildings that protect and reinforce the stand of giant fir trees while accommodating the hybrid design that's in harmony with the site.

FACING PAGE BOTTOM LEFT: The material palette for the raw concrete guest house is inspired by the rocky beaches that form the site's shifting boundaries. Here, a window detail forms a solstice clock set to the angle of the setting summer solstice sun.

FACING PAGE BOTTOM RIGHT: Despite the extensive use of glass, the home is virtually energy-neutral through the integration of a 7K-watt solar array plus the heavy thermal mass of exposed concrete structural walls, allowing it to be grid-independent in the event of major storms.
Photographs by Andrew Dunbar, INTERSTICE Architects

"What inspires us most is honoring a site and operating from an atmosphere of stewardship and ecological sensitivity."
—Andrew Dunbar

ABOVE LEFT: We drew inspiration for this custom fireplace from a storm lantern. It also holds the speakers for the drop-down projection screen above and provides wood storage for the fire—all while balancing the weight of the concrete plinth that emerges from the floor below.

ABOVE RIGHT: We like to call this the sunrise kitchen—it catches the sun's rays each morning and its vivid blood-orange color resonates across the entire space. Wood cladding conceals the refrigerator and freezer and extends outwards through the glass wall to the exterior garden kitchen beyond.
Photographs by Brad Laughton

BOTTOM: The signature, verdant green hue continues from the exterior of the home upwards into the heart of the house and then through the corridor linking the two volumes. The vibrant shade works as a chromatic orientation device all the way through the entire space.
Photograph by Andrew Dunbar, INTERSTICE Architects

FACING PAGE TOP: The two-story living room is richly connected to the outdoors via natural wood tones and vibrant, saturated colors, each uniquely echoed from the surrounding forest.

FACING PAGE BOTTOM: No need for art when the views are an ever-changing wonder, seen in their full majesty with glass walls that slide open onto the deck. The living area is a giant aperture framing both the Canadian Rockies eastward across the Georgia Straight and the island's coastal wetlands to the west.
Photographs by Brad Laughton

BELOW & FACING PAGE: Hillside Modern is a private residence located on the western front of the Bridger Range, just north of Bozeman. While located only a few minutes from town, this site is decidedly in the mountain environment. The design team, led by architect Shea Stewart, worked to create a strategy for mountain living, capturing the dramatic views of the surrounding landscape while also providing a level of intimacy within the exposed site. The resulting design established a hierarchy of spaces that respond accordingly and fashion an engaged living experience.
Photographs by Derik Olsen Photography

Intrinsik Architecture

Over the past 20 years, Intrinsik Architecture has evolved from founder Dan Harding's one-person, garage-based operation into a full-service architecture and planning firm providing services throughout Montana and the surrounding region. Based in Bozeman, principals Tad Tsukamoto and Robert Pertzborn have encountered their fair share of challenges in promoting contemporary architecture in an area sometimes seen as relatively rural. Continued vision, optimism, and perseverance has led to Intrinsik's emergence as one of the state's leading design firms.

From single and multi-household residences, to mixed-use commercial, and civic buildings, as well as land use planning, Intrinsik has distinguished itself as a community-based design studio emphasizing projects that embody and preserve the spirit of its clients and place.

BELOW TOP: The exposed exterior concrete retaining wall was carried through the interior of the house, reinforcing the connection between the interior and exterior.

BELOW BOTTOM: The more intimate views of the Bridger Range were best experienced by forming a semi-enclosed courtyard, using the house and mountains to define the exterior living room.
Photographs by Derik Olsen Photography

BELOW: The high ceilings, open floor plan, and glazed walls provide a light-filled space with 180-degree views from the Bridger Range to the Gallatin Valley.
Photographs by Derik Olsen Photography

"Of all the design challenges, using restraint might be the most difficult and perhaps the most admirable."
—Shea Stewart

FACING PAGE TOP, CENTER & BOTTOM: An emphasis has been placed on blending indoor and outdoor spaces to create a seamless and comfortable transition between the interior and exterior living spaces. The kitchen and dining room open to a private courtyard, enclosed by a detached garage and integrated privacy screening.

BELOW: The Parkside Infill consists of simple and classic forms clad in cedar siding, which provides a natural and warm texture, tactility, and scale to the home. The project was designed to fit within and respond to the eclectic character of Northeast Bozeman, and provides a contemporary and sustainable take on traditional western single-family architecture.
Photographs by Derik Olsen Photography

BELOW TOP: A small footprint and the efficient use of space lead to an open floor plan that is organized to provide a range of public and private spaces. These spaces allow residents the opportunity to engage with park users and neighbors outside on two levels, or to retreat into the quiet solitude of their home and sheltered courtyard. The high ceilings and open stair enlarge the living room without increasing the overall footprint of the house.

BELOW BOTTOM: A built-in library and office open to the living room below.

FACING PAGE: The exterior living spaces transition from neighborhood connected social spaces on the street side to a secluded courtyard hidden from the public view. The master bedroom opens to a private, second-story deck.
Photographs by Derik Olsen Photography

BELOW: A true original, Residence 1 presents a vibrant visual narrative where water—the majesty of Lake Washington—plays the muse. We wanted the design theme to echo the lake's movement, from the undulating roofline's curvilinear forms to the repeated arcs throughout. The home's vantage points also enable sweeping views of the lake, Mt. Rainier, and the city of Bellevue. The interior's flow of space and harmony of textures likewise celebrate the sweeping vistas while connecting the inside seamlessly to the outdoors.
Photograph by David Papazian

FACING PAGE: Visual intrigue abounds everywhere the eye falls in Residence 2, an 18,000-square-foot artisanal contemporary family home. We wanted the dramatic entryway, with its fire and stone elements, to be a sneak peek into the artistic energy that lies ahead.
Photograph by Ethan Kaminsky

KHA Architects

A tremendous culture of positive creativity infuses the work of KHA Architects; that means exploration is encouraged, and so is pushing the envelope. In fact, it's the essence of the full-service architecture and interior design firm's practice. Their belief in experimentation gives rise to ideas that might not otherwise have been considered—and that's where the magic begins.

Founder Kristi Hanson and her team design homes that are original but that are also a reflection of their owners; it's both a challenge and an exciting adventure. The firm is widely recognized for its ability to create visually arresting, inviting, and comfortable properties.

KHA Architects' design work is a blend of intuition and innovation, artistry and engineering—and their highly individual residences ultimately enhance people's lives. The team is passionate about transforming their clients' aspirations into statement-making, functional homes while maintaining a reputation for fresh, original structures that overcome site-specific challenges. Again and again, clients say that the firm honors and incorporates their most deeply held ideas of home—in a way they never could have imagined.

Although the firm is forward-thinking, their work is never at the expense of the environment. Their goal is to harmonize with and preserve the area's natural character to yield beautiful, sound architecture that respects and complements the surrounding environment and geography.

BELOW TOP: Everything about Residence 2 is oriented to the superb desert views, with the home wrapping around mountain and water views to embrace the site. To take full advantage of the natural environment, we designed an extensive outdoor living space with dining areas and seating pods that overlook an infinity pool.

BELOW BOTTOM: Creative energy abounds across the exterior of Residence 2, creating a dynamic entrance for the homeowners, thanks to the use of mixed materials including stucco, stone, and metal as well as curved and linear forms.
Photographs by Ethan Kaminsky

BELOW TOP: We balanced the cooler elements of the glossy, reflecting water and stonework with amber warmth radiating from within Residence 2 thanks to teakwood, ambient lighting, and an outdoor fireplace.

BELOW BOTTOM: This sketch of Residence 1's first floor offers a view of the main living space's dual seating areas that create informal places to gather and relax.
Photographs by Ethan Kaminsky

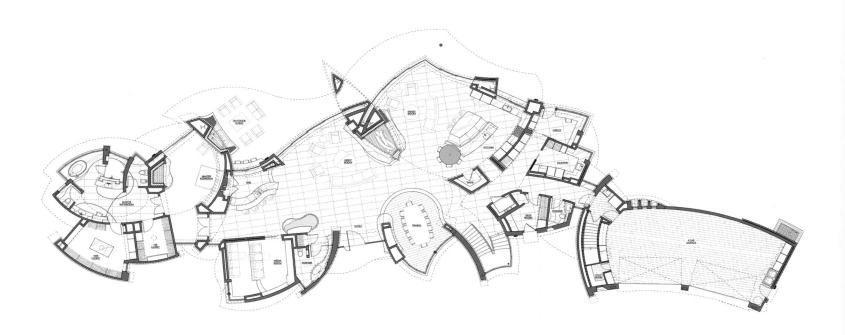

FIRST FLOOR PLAN

BELOW TOP: Artistry meets contemporary design in Residence 3 where both innovation and luxury collide. We set the stage for dynamic drama from the first sight of the copper roofline with its curvilinear edge contrasting the adjacent straight lines.

BELOW BOTTOM: The curves and geometric forms of Residence 3 read like an awe-inspiring sculpture—one that the homeowners get to live in.
Photographs by Ethan Kaminsky

"Creating architecture that embodies and imparts the desires of the people who will live there in a beautiful, evocative, and deeply personal way is one of the things that inspires us most."
—Kristi Hanson

BELOW TOP: The rear elevation of Residence 3 showcases a curved roofline structure that ends in a bold point, evoking rhythm and movement. To repeat the allure of the arc, we carved the outdoor bar from a single stone to offer a vantage point for sweeping views. The two extraordinary pools and three spas elevate the joy of outdoor living, as does a stainless grill paired with a stone table for easy alfresco dining.

BELOW BOTTOM: Quarry-cut granite on the walls and oversized slabs of travertine on the floors make for a captivating interplay of natural materials. Multiple fireplaces, both inside and out—as well as the fire sculptures we placed in the back by the small pool— emit light and warmth for cool desert evenings.
Photographs by David Blank

BELOW TOP: An artful take on modernity, Residence 4 leads an exuberant dual existence—the home is at once smooth yet textural; sumptuous yet simple; innovative yet inviting. In essence, the architecture's clean lines and sophisticated minimalism let it speak for itself. We designed every aspect of this home, both inside and out, to be seamlessly integrated, including the inspired main living area that features custom furnishings and a wine bar that's well-suited for entertaining or quiet luxury.

BELOW BOTTOM: Residence 4's magical outdoor setting boasts a mix of cushioned seating, water features, a fireplace, and a dining area—plus a cooking and grill zone. Just inside, the kitchen's polished cabinets fuse sleek, transparent surfaces with rich mahogany and clear Quartzite counters. The property's synthesis of color and character responds to the evolving play of natural light.
Photographs by Ethan Kaminsky

BELOW TOP: Simultaneously elegant and organic, Residence 5 features a zinc-clad front elevation. We also used wood and stone to nod to the home's natural elements. Wide glass expanses blur the line between indoors and out— s do the extensive outdoor seating areas that enhance shared experiences between family and friends.

BELOW BOTTOM: Residence 5's blend of luxe and natural surfaces radiate tranquil harmony, as seen here in the outdoor water feature that welcomes you to the front entry.
Photographs by Ethan Kaminsky

"At its core, architecture is creative, inspiring and optimistic. It's about what's possible."
—Kristi Hanson

BELOW TOP: The seamless integration of exterior and interior expands the living space and brings the landscape into the residence. The hilltop setting with vanishing-edge pool creates an illusion of a waterfall into the ravine. Conversation areas abound with a natural stone fire pit along with a covered TV and fireplace in this outdoor room.

BELOW CENTER: Layers of sleek yet warm materials in the kitchen are highlighted by golden lightening granite countertops, glass tile backsplash, and walnut cabinets. An onyx console is illuminated to provide a separation between the kitchen and dining area.

BELOW BOTTOM: A strong linear fireplace is highlighted with the use of a light shell stone against the textured grand tortoise limestone, uniting the interior with the exterior. The focus of the room is the outside views to the mountains at the front and the lower valley from the pool area.
Photographs by Ethan Kaminsky

BELOW: Nestled into a mountain site, this 6,500-square-foot home features sweeping views of a natural ravine and the city below. The textural, desert-hued grand tortoise limestone creates a oneness with the mountain landscape. The angular metal roof accentuates the mountain views and forms.
Photograph by Ethan Kaminsky

BELOW & FACING PAGE: The three levels of this home are entirely visible due to the main eye-catcher: an aircraft hangar door used as a glass curtain wall that extends the living experience outdoors. A cantilevered dining room sits atop an indoor-outdoor swimming pool with Michelangelo's *The Creation of Adam* in the mosaic-tiled floor. *Photographs by Scott DuBose*

M•Designs Architects

Growing up, Malika Junaid used to travel to Europe every year with her family and was fascinated by the different varieties of architecture she encountered. That love of unique design combined perfectly with her natural artistic tendencies, and Junaid learned, as she continued to travel, that architecture can define an entire culture and civilization. Today, she and her colleagues at the award-winning M•Designs Architects never lose sight of the importance of function and enduring beauty when crafting sustainable, residential designs.

Together with co-founder Alpheus Jessup, Junaid delivers more than 45 years of design and management experience in the architecture world along with an impressive resume of accolades. In 2009, she founded Green Learning Institute in California, which helped communities establish environmentally sustainable building practices through ongoing training and education.

The next year, she co-founded the Pakistan Green Building Council, a nonprofit organization committed to promoting sustainable concepts and practices to transform the way buildings and communities are built and operated in her native Pakistan.

The team at M•Designs is known for their exemplary listening skills and empathetic approach which ensures that each project is tailored to the client's unique needs and wants.

BELOW TOP: The modern kitchen features a nineteen-foot cantilevered island, a turquoise moving glass backsplash, and sleek, modern appliances with touch and sensor-enabled cabinets and lighting system.

BELOW BOTTOM: The residence opens with a fifteen-foot entrance door into the great room. A glass wall to the garage is on one side, with a winding stainless-steel staircase, a suspended stainless-steel bridge with a glass walkway, and a Star Trek-inspired circular glass elevator as the technical wonder in the middle.
Photographs by Peter Giles

BELOW: The turquoise of the mosaic-floored pool and red accents provide splashes of color to the white home. The bocce court is an elegant entertainment area while the majestic olive tree balances nature and the high-tech suburban home.
Landscape Architect: dhd Damir Hurdich design
Photograph by Scott DuBose

BELOW: Each level has floor-to-ceiling glass that maximizes panoramic views of the Silicon Valley hills and protected Coastal oak trees. The dark hardwood floors stand out against the white background.

FACING PAGE: Built on a challenging slope, the residence is designed in three levels distinguishing different areas as well as being sensitive to the slope. The multi-level design complements its natural surroundings, and each level is split to create separate environments, like the lounging, vegetation, and swimming areas, respectively.
Photographs by Peter Giles

"Traveling opens up your eyes to how the world is perceived."
—Malika Junaid

"*Never compromise on the first impression.*"
—Malika Junaid

BELOW: The backyard is the epitome of outdoor living and entertaining with a lap pool, jacuzzi, outdoor kitchen, and basketball court. Carefully selected lighting accentuates the residence's best features.

FACING PAGE TOP: A double-height ceiling and wall-to-wall windows bring in views of the pool and hills beyond. An abstract, three-piece artwork on the wall brings in the colors of the pool inside.

FACING PAGE BOTTOM: The dining room and lounge are divided by a double-sided glass fireplace while a glass wall ensures the entire view can be enjoyed at any time of the day.
Landscape Architect: dhd Damir Hurdich design
Photographs by Scott DuBose

BELOW & FACING PAGE: Kayak House is a 3,700-square-foot home that I designed for an avid kayaker and his wife. They wanted a weekend retreat dedicated to the kayak and the river. It's located on the South Fork of the American River overlooking one of the best kayak runs in Northern California. The site is four-and-a-half acres, only a few miles from where gold was discovered in 1848. The 25-foot-high living room faces upriver, offering an ever-changing tableau of kayaks and rafts drifting past, while the 35-foot-high dining room faces the owner's private kayak launch.
Photographs by Tim Griffith

Maria Ogrydziak Architecture

For Maria Ogrydziak, architecture is like painting—Chinese brush painting, to be exact. The goal is to make a cohesive whole from separate elements, each piece with its own set of dynamics. You must think holistically, but carefully identify each part and know its role.

Maria has always loved to paint, but it wasn't until her father's engineering career took the family to Taiwan that she fell in love with Chinese brush painting. Without a Western equivalent, the practice held an intrigue for Maria. She saw the beautiful connection between the brain, the hands, and the resulting piece of work—none of which were possible without the other. It opened up a whole new world of creation. Every inflection, every movement, every thought plays into the elements that create the final product; nothing is accidental and everything works in harmony. This craft has stayed with Maria and carried her into her work as an architect, and even as a sculptor. Maria's sculptures have been exhibited at the Oakland Museum.

After graduating from the Massachusetts Institute of Technology where she was student body president, Maria founded her namesake California firm in 1985. Here, she became well-known for her valley-inspired designs. And although every project has a distinct sense of the California landscape, Maria is continually inspired by her years of traveling. Born in Stockholm to Estonian parents, she lived in Canada and Taipei, Taiwan, before landing in Davis, California. Each of these cultures have had a distinct influence on her more than 400 residential, retail, and worship spaces.

"Once a successful project is complete, the structure seems so natural on its site, but the amount of problem-solving behind every design is both intricate and massive. Built works are a marvel in critical thinking."
—Maria Ogrydziak

BELOW & FACING PAGE: I situated the house as close to the river as possible, five feet above the 100-year flood-line. I organized the plan to focus on two important kayak-related site features: the rapids and the launch. The living room is constructed of earth-colored, split-face masonry, and the dining room is clad in gold-colored Douglas fir. The first floor follows the terrain of the riverbank, resulting in a two-level space that emphasizes the large river views. The house is designed for aging in place, and the levels are connected with a wheelchair ramp, integrated into the terraced aesthetic of the interior. The living room can serve as a bedroom, allowing a view of the river from the bed, and the picture window acts as a movie screen to capture the constantly changing natural world and the riverbank outside. The view from this oversized, 18-foot-high window permeates life inside the home, as it can be enjoyed from multiple interior spaces including the living room, dining room, kitchen, and second-floor study. Inside, exposed angled-steel framing and large-scale wood mullions suggest a texture of interior branches and act as an extension of the natural world inside the house.
Photographs by Tim Griffith

LEFT, ABOVE & FACING PAGE: My task for Flight House was to design a single-family, live-work home in the agricultural California Central Valley countryside in the Pacific Flyway. Located just 10 minutes away from town, this 2,800-square-foot custom homestead was an opportunity for a couple to bring back childhood memories of playing in far-flung meadows and to bring them to life for their young son.

The house is a Central Valley adaptation of the Case Study Houses of Pierre Koenig. Working more than 60 years ago, Koenig's vision for affordable contemporary living—providing modernity and elegance together with privacy and openness—is applicable today. I made the most of the client's modest budget to create a contemporary, regionally inspired house that captures the diurnal cycle, tracking the sun's path from sunrise to sunset. Its architectural language takes cues from the expansive valley sky, long views, and circadian rhythms of the site, and the structural wings pay homage to the hundreds of bird species that travel the Pacific Flyway, as well as the planes that crisscross the sky far above. Tall folding glass doors open the corners of the house to the exterior when the weather allows, seamlessly connecting the interior and the land. It builds on the heritage of California modernism, but is constructed of materials that have been adapted to be more energy efficient and livable in the Central Valley desert climate.
Photographs by Julia Ogrydziak

BELOW: On my first visit to the site of Flow House, situated at the western edge of California's Central Valley, I was awestruck by the immense scale of the view down and across the valley. The feeling of flowing and endless open space became the primary theme in the house's design. This 2,600-square-foot rural house was built for a professional couple with two grown children. The north façade engages the landscape through a series of folded vertical planes whose angles emphasize different views from both floors. Thirty-foot walls of windows connect the house interior to the exterior fields and sky, and the building materials work in harmony with the surrounding terrain.
Photographs by Luke Ogrydziak and Tom Bonner

BELOW: In many ways, the central living space resembles a large gallery. With the exterior views as the primary attraction inside, the architecture enacts a series of gallery display conventions; All walls are painted a modernist white, a niche cut between the stairs allows for sculpture display; and the great room walls are comfortably sized for hanging large, abstract paintings. The only significant breakdown of the purity of this whiteness is the living room floor. Its color matches the green lawn outside, blurring the interior-exterior boundary through an optical extension of the central space to the grass and fields outside.
Photographs by Luke Ogrydziak and Tom Bonner

BELOW: I wanted to design an urban oasis that would be at once a working artist's studio and a place to relax and entertain, so I created Edge Loft. This new 1,500-square-foot space was added to a 100-year-old bungalow in a block of downtown Davis that marked the transition between the commercial core and the surrounding residential neighborhoods.

FACING PAGE: Recognizing that traditional and contemporary spaces are different in character but can coexist and be mutually enlivening, I sliced and punched the bungalow to make way for a 20-foot threshold that threads both spaces. Where I removed existing windows, I framed the openings in blue-stained wood, marking the connections between old and new. Where former exterior walls became interior walls of the loft, I further illuminated the relation between the two eras by exposing the bungalow's original wood sheathing. I left much of the new construction exposed, including steel web ceiling trusses, steel columns, and a concrete slab floor—adding texture and serving as a commentary on the underlying design and construction.
Photographs by Jay Graham and Julia Ogrydziak

*"Art is a window
to the world."*
—Maria Ogrydziak

BELOW: Originally a mid-century home that we redesigned, T r House in Woodside, California is a study in the harmony of dualities. The house itself unites Japanese and mid-century modernist aesthetics while fully integrating its natural hillside surroundings with a redwood forest grove to the east and a deciduous grove and meadow to the west. The homeowner, being a true renaissance man—product designer, software engineer, and playwright—loved the site for its transformative nature and the choreography of moving through it.

FACING PAGE: The homeowner's aesthetic is grounded in the essence of all things Japanese, which inspired the design. Deeply cantilevered flat roof planes cover decks, at once controlling the sun's rays into the house while creating transitional indoor and outdoor living spaces. We wanted to accentuate the feeling of the home being perched above the ground in the canopy of redwoods.
Photographs by Bruce Damonte

Mark English Architects

When Mark English, AIA, was a young child, he wanted to be an archaeologist, fascinated by puzzling out the intentions of past civilizations by pondering artifacts. Ultimately, he found it more interesting to create artifacts.

Now, as principal of Mark English Architects, he is doing just that, providing beautifully tailored homes, work, and entertainment spaces since 1992 and offering a designer's sense of artistry supported by practical knowledge gained from years of hands-on building experience.

His practice is built on providing design that is sustainable because it is sensible and flexible; design that's shaped by the place where it's found rather than a particular style. Mark and his team believe a room needs to be memorable—by virtue of a distinctive shape or volume, or even a type of material. He's also inspired by his love of travel and experiencing how different cultures live and how they've worked their own buildings into the landscape—particularly in Japan, Peru, and Italy.

Interestingly, Mark English Architects offices in the 1940 former studio of sculptors Robert Howard and Adaline Kent, which is perfect for their practice as it's full of natural light and is logical and beautifully sculpted for its use—much like the firm's own work.

BELOW: The home's interior, including the streamlined kitchen, is uniformly peaceful in soft white, accommodating the owner's furnishings and favorite objects.

FACING PAGE TOP & CENTER: The open floor plan allows for the kitchen to open directly into the main living area, which echoes the calm, white color palette with carefully considered pops of pink and purple hues integrated throughout.The clear finished cedar siding that covers the entire exterior of the building also wraps back under the eaves onto the dining room ceiling to create a sense of continuity between the interior and exterior.

FACING PAGE BOTTOM: The floors throughout the home are mostly muted porcelain and travertine tiles, accented occasionally by the introduction of warm teak wood, as in the master bathroom.
Photographs by Bruce Damonte

BELOW & FACING PAGE: Exciting curb appeal and a proven floorplan are hallmarks of this modern, two-story house. There is a covered outdoor living space directly adjacent to the kitchen, dining, and great room—the home is the epitome of open-concept.
Interiors by Straightline Design
Photographs by Dan Francis

Mark Stewart Home Design

Mark Stewart has been designing homes most of his life, inspired by a lifelong love of art, design, and the work of Frank Lloyd Wright, Christopher Alexander, Richard Neutra, and Ralph Lauren, among others. He began as an architectural drafting student at Estacada High School—even designing the façade of the new Estacada Admin building in 1975—before being offered full-ride scholarships to an array of colleges. After studying architecture at the University of Oregon and Portland State, Stewart left early to gain practical experience.

At the age of 30, and directly coincident with taking formal vows as a spiritual practitioner of The Way of The Heart-Adidam, Stewart's design work, creativity, and intuition took a vast leap forward. Within a very short time, he was producing some of the hottest designs in the country and quickly amassed a loyal following of leading developers and homebuilders, including the highest profile custom home commissions. Starting in 2007, Stewart became a guest designer for *Extreme Makeover: Home Edition* on ABC, and in 2010, the firm began the process of recreating the "full-service design experience" for its clients. The cutting-edge team provides the finest in photorealistic rendering and 3-D technology, so clients can feel fully immersed in their new home prior to building it.

BELOW & FACING PAGE: A central light core window arrangement near the top of the great room ceiling floods the home with daylight. A gourmet kitchen is truly the center of the home while the bedrooms are afforded privacy through wings for guests and children and the master suite situated at the rear of the home. The home also includes a large pool room and fitness center, complete with its own bathroom, behind the oversized two-car garage.
Interiors by Straightline Design
Photographs by Dan Francis

BELOW: This elegant home is a natural-light-lover's dream, creating a captivating harmony of light and space. Its limitless possibilities include a daylight basement option, multi-car garage, and array of outdoor living spaces with the possibility of a built-in fireplace.

FACING PAGE: The great room is a dynamic living space with 16-foot ceilings and plenty of windows. Upstairs is a spacious bonus room that functions as the ideal playroom or media room.
Photographs by Bria Huffman

"Sometimes an exciting mix of chaos, melody, and purpose are needed to achieve the perfect house plan."
—Mark Stewart

BELOW & FACING PAGE: Incredible views were the priority for this custom contemporary home, with three stories of windows providing vistas from the rear of the home. A three-car garage was carefully integrated to enhance the roofline and provide even more interesting angles. Inside, the main floor embraces an open-concept kitchen, dining, and great room with wide-open yet still intimate spaces.
Photographs by David Pappazian

"What can start as a folded and crumpled origami-like piece of paper can end up as a beautiful, organic, modern design."
—Mark Stewart

BELOW & FACING PAGE: On the lower floor, you'll find four spacious bedrooms along with a large recreation room and two full baths. The master suite is situated at the rear of the upper floor, with a spacious deck of its own and a retreat space near the luxurious bath. A two-story, invigorating atrium is situated right off the dining room with the master suite above.
Photographs by David Pappazian

BELOW & FACING PAGE: The architecture of *Suncatch* came about after an eight year design and construction process. It sits on 30 acres in a sought-after area of Southern California known as Rancho Santa Fe. Mr. Applebaum's clients told him that they wanted the finest home in the region. This request became this architect's thesis. The architect wanted the roof and its cantilevered beams to defy gravity, which they did. The appearance reflects a roof that is floating. The gable terracotta roof tiles (below left) were designed by Mr. Applebaum.
Photographs by Mary E. Nichols

Norm Applebaum Architect

Norm Applebaum has made his name a pillar in the world of California architecture by focusing on two simple elements: the client and the architecture. His buildings possess distinct forms and without duplication. His dream is to create something beautiful, a work of art, without sacrificing the home's functionality. "If the home doesn't function for my clients, it isn't architecture," Mr. Applebaum states.

Architecture, and everything that goes into it, is a way of life for this architect. Studying space is the essence of his craft, and he firmly believes that any architect who designs solely on paper or computer with no study model, will never create an intelligent building. Architecture is a holistic entity, it's all-encompassing. Mentored by the late Calvin Straub, FAIA, Norm graduated in 1968 from the College of Architecture at Arizona State University in Tempe, Arizona, and was influenced by the late Cliff May, father of the California Ranch House. He learned from both the importance of the site and its surroundings, and how to integrate those elements into a home's design. Many of Mr. Applebaum's thoughts come from his background as a jazz trombonist, relying on creativity and improvisation that was honed many years ago. "The ability to improvise jazz freely and generate original ideas correlates directly with my architectural process."

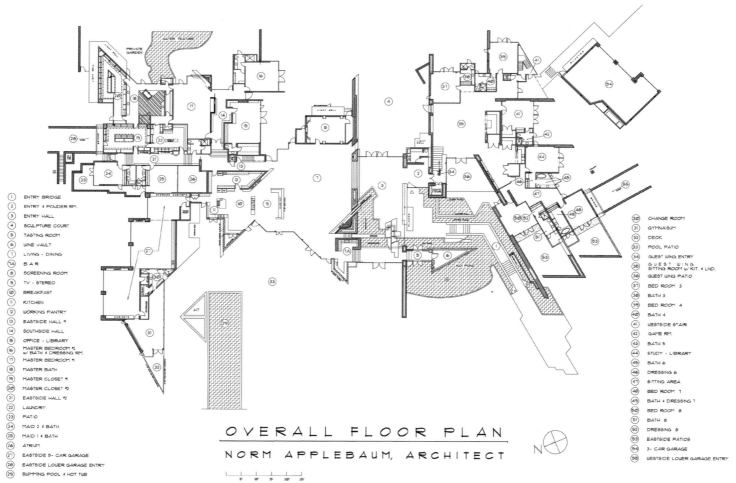

1. ENTRY BRIDGE
2. ENTRY & POWDER RM.
3. ENTRY HALL
4. SCULPTURE COURT
5. TASTING ROOM
6. WINE VAULT
7. LIVING - DINING
7A. BAR
8. SCREENING ROOM
9. TV - STEREO
10. BREAKFAST
11. KITCHEN
12. WORKING PANTRY
13. EASTSIDE HALL #1
14. SOUTHSIDE HALL
15. OFFICE - LIBRARY
16. MASTER BEDROOM #2 w/ BATH & DRESSING RM.
17. MASTER BEDROOM #1
18. MASTER BATH
19. MASTER CLOSET #1
20. MASTER CLOSET #2
21. EASTSIDE HALL #2
22. LAUNDRY
23. PATIO
24. MAID 2 & BATH
25. MAID 1 & BATH
26. ATRIUM
27. EASTSIDE 5- CAR GARAGE
28. EASTSIDE LOWER GARAGE ENTRY
29. SWIMMING POOL & HOT TUB

30. CHANGE ROOM
31. GYMNASIUM
32. DECK
33. POOL PATIO
34. GUEST WING ENTRY
35. GUEST WING SITTING ROOM w/ KIT. & LND.
36. GUEST WING PATIO
37. BED ROOM 3
38. BATH 3
39. BED ROOM 4
40. BATH 4
41. WESTSIDE STAIR
42. GAME RM.
43. BATH 5
44. STUDY - LIBRARY
45. BATH 6
46. DRESSING 6
47. SITTING AREA
48. BED ROOM 7
49. BATH & DRESSING 7
50. BED ROOM 8
51. BATH 8
52. DRESSING 8
53. EASTSIDE PATIOS
54. 3- CAR GARAGE
55. WESTSIDE LOWER GARAGE ENTRY

OVERALL FLOOR PLAN
NORM APPLEBAUM, ARCHITECT

N

BELOW TOP: The home's views are to the north yet large overhangs were used to capture the south sun and brighten up the interior spaces, hence Mr. Applebaum named the project *Suncatch*.
Photograph by Mary E. Nichols

FACING PAGE: The project consists of 54,000 square feet of floor space. Of that, 24,500 square feet is for living space and 29,500 square feet is for a 37-car showroom under the house. The Southern California estate was finished in 2005. The late Julius Shulman, famed architectural photographer, stated at the open house of *Suncatch* in 2005, that "This home is the greatest residential architecture of the 21st century."
Aerial photograph by Paul Barnett

LEFT: Norm Applebaum, architect of *Suncatch*
Photograph by Martin Mann

RIGHT: Chuck Lang, general contractor of *Suncatch*
Photograph by Teri Lang

BELOW: To reach the entry of the home, one actually drives through the pool structure with water cascading down the side walls and open to the sky above. All roads are finished in hand-cut Italian porphyry stone.

FACING PAGE: The architect designed the home by model only, no two-dimensional drawings were used except the floor plan. This gave him time to study each space and learn what is proper and relative to human scale for each room in the house. Working drawings were created after totally scaling the study model. Mr. Applebaum designed all of the leaded-glass art throughout the house; one has to experience it in person to grasp how impactful it is.
Photographs by Mary E. Nichols

"Studying space, and form, is the essence of architecture and a way of life for me, I never tire of its infinite possibilities."
—Norm Applebaum

BELOW: Lighting and niches are used to showcase and highlight works of art and sculpture. Shelves and overhangs move through fixed glass and beyond to extend space, as in the living room and the master bedroom below . The architect wanted to create a feeling that the spaces in the home were totally unified and that it became a sculptural work of art.
Photographs by Mary E. Nichols

BELOW: Water features throughout the interior and exterior add an additional level of sensory experience. Chuck Lang, the general contractor, purchased a half-million board feet of clear vertical grain Douglas fir from a lumber mill in Oregon—depleting their stock for this project. Douglas fir was used throughout the residence; this includes the floors, ceilings, cabinets, doors, built-up fascia, and all the trim. Plaster walls and poured-in-place concrete, using a veneer system that Mr. Applebaum invented, are the outcome. The architecture possesses a strong sense of openness with plenty of natural light.
Photographs by Mary E. Nichols

BELOW: To create clean lines, Mr. Applebaum does not use moldings, but prefers reveals between surfaces that define and visually separate materials. The result is a shadow line that enhances the details of the architecture. All stairs in the home are designed with monumental rise and two-foot-deep cantilevered treads and almost seem to float and have an organic look to them. Flooding the spaces in light, the materials show off their rich color and aesthetic appeal.
Photographs by Mary E. Nichols

"Norm Applebaum's work is tied to the Modernists of Southern California—Harris, Shindler, Wright—yet it is fresh, new, and exciting."
—Julius Shulman, 2005

BELOW: The architect uses the exterior of a home as other rooms and other spaces which provide many interesting possibilities. The integration with the site and its landscaped surroundings was so important that the use of wood and organic materials was essential to stay in harmony with the land. Southern California's Rancho Santa Fe is one of the most beautiful places in the country, so the architect had every reason to highlight the environment.
Photographs by Mary E. Nichols

BELOW: When my team and I designed the Ancient Cedars chalet for a young international couple with young kids, we wanted to capture their sophisticated taste and modern style without losing any functionality. The home has big bones, with tall weathering beams, and utilizes cedar and glass to achieve its West Coast appeal. Large windows help take advantage of the views, and generous overhangs protect the home from heavy snow and rain.

FACING PAGE: The massive window system allows natural light to pour in and shows off the beauty of concrete juxtaposed with steel. The fireplace is a focal point in the family room, and its mast acts as the central column for the home's structure, anchoring the entire design.
Photographs by Ema Peter Photography

Openspace Architecture

Openspace Architecture embraces the old and the new and allows these two elements to constantly work together. Founded by principal Don Gurney, the boutique Vancouver-based firm utilizes a process with both modern and traditional components. All projects begin with a pen and paper, then progress to an integrated design process that incorporates all disciplines and building elements into one cohesive digital 3-D model. That same blending of old and new can be found in Openspace's finished projects. The designs possess a modern beauty and usability, but have the old-fashioned comfort and familiar materials that homeowners love.

The firm takes a playful, rigorous approach to design, where collaboration is key. Clients and consultants always feel welcome and appreciated, and the Openspace creative team offers an invaluable experience. Openspace specializes in single-family and resort residential projects, but also has a broad range of experience in master planning and infrastructure projects. And although the firm is based on Canada's west coast, that hasn't stopped them from taking on projects around the world. Always moved and inspired by different cultures, the team enjoys international projects. It's a chance to engage with new challenges and a variety of styles. Don believes that extraordinary design feels as though it was simply meant to be, an expression of its inhabitants, the environment, and the spaces in between—no matter where it is in the world.

BELOW: Board-form concrete, rusted steel beams, and a slick modern kitchen make for a robust yet refined look. The floor plan was made for large family gatherings, with the kitchen as the center of all the activity.

FACING PAGE: The Ancient Cedars chalet has several sustainable elements, including the use of all reclaimed timber from a warehouse. Made of recycled steel, the stairs are reclaimable—should the house ever come down in the future.
Photographs by Ema Peter Photography

"The homes I design have a strong emphasis on nature and surrounding views."
—Don Gurney

BELOW & FACING PAGE: The site of this Whistler residence very much dictates the design, and in this case, we built the home to work with its tall narrow lot. Positioned to hang out over the valley, the house opens up as it descends downward. The discreet entrance is on a half level and has a beautifully understated appeal among the lush foliage.
Photographs by Russell Dalby

BELOW: I incorporate views of the mountains and trees whenever possible. A corner sitting area in the master bedroom has floor-to-ceiling glass. With the frame recessed into the floor, the windows make it seem like the exterior is part of the inside of the room. The entry foyer in the home shows has the same feeling, with crisp outdoor views.

FACING PAGE: This modern Whistler residence embodies all the comfort that you'd imagine in a ski home, and every room has the same feeling of camping—but with a magical quality. The oval-shaped fireplace provides traditional warmth, adds visual interest to the living room, and acts as a counterpoint. It also has a structural purpose, as it forms a seismic anchor and supports the house's lateral loads.
Photographs by Russell Dalby

"Our work is driven by a deep respect for the relationships between people, nature, and the built environment."
—Don Gurney

"Teamwork is integral to everything we do."
—Don Gurney

ABOVE & LEFT: The Lighthouse residence sits in Nelson, British Colombia, on the banks of Kootenay Lake. Because of the natural beauty of the site, we used materials that would enhance and reflect the surroundings. Ipe windows protect the interior of the home from the elements of lakeside living while still maintaining a strong outdoor connection.

FACING PAGE: We consulted with a wide range of specialists, including local copper and window artisans. The teamwork paid off beautifully, as seen through the extensive window design that allows for tons of natural light and the copper details found throughout the home. The kitchen's warmth comes from the natural light and materials used to build the home. *Photographs by Karen Redfern*

BELOW: This home is a defining property within the Big Sky, Montana region; it was one of the first to push the boundaries of interior spaces and exterior landscape. Large apertures of glass frame the views of Pioneer Mountain and Cedar Mountain to the west. A stone axial wall offers an integral design feature of the home, creating a backdrop for the great room while separating the public spaces from the private areas. In exploring the site during the schematic stages of design, the firm stumbled upon a linear outcropping of stone, which was playfully developed into a key design element of the home.

FACING PAGE: Although the home has more than 9,000 square feet of living space, its careful integration with the hillside along with the preservation of trees gives the residence the intended appearance of a much smaller residence. The firm lowered its visual presence and tucked it more quietly into the landscape. The slight roof pitch to the north allows for a view up to the summit of Lone Mountain. The simple and direct building forms divulge our inspiration: Mies Van Der Rohe's less-is-more approach to design.
Photographs by Roger Wade Studios

Reid Smith Architects

Reid Smith Architects has spent the better part of the last decade as a driving force in redefining mountain architecture, where principal architects Reid Smith and Daryl Nourse are pushing the boundaries between traditional western architecture and modern, clean design. The firm creates unconventionally stunning, responsive projects across the United States that likewise reflect the beauty of their diverse, dynamic environments. At the beginning of any project, they seek to find something on site that serves as unique inspiration to define the site. Indeed, it is often the awe-inspiring landscapes in which their clients live that truly influence Reid Smith Architects' work, as they echo and complement the exterior surroundings throughout the design with the use of both local and natural materials.

With a collaborative process between client, architect, contractor, and consultant, the firm ensures that innovative, forward-thinking ideas are brought to fruition. Whether it's a minimalist, contemporary cabin on the Yellowstone River, a western ski retreat, or a modern mountain residence, the diverse portfolio of Reid Smith Architects continues to beautifully capture the spirit of the site.

BELOW TOP: The home feels like it's floating in the trees. The linear design of the residence allows for a number of bedrooms and ancillary spaces below, providing a strong base for the great room and master wing to hover above the evergreens.

BELOW BOTTOM: An open floor plan along a large expanse of glass allows for each of the spaces in the main living and dining area to share a view.

FACING PAGE TOP: Opposite the view, a backdrop was created of reclaimed barnwood. To soften the surfaces, natural regional materials are often incorporated. They add interest and warmth, and become the view after the sun sets.

FACING PAGE BOTTOM: A stair leads down to the ski room while capturing the view of the chutes on Pioneer, the most extreme terrain on the mountain.
Photographs by Roger Wade Studios

"Melding the interior with the exterior creates a visceral connection to nature and a sense of ease."
—Daryl Nourse

BELOW: This lake house sits comfortably within a lusciously treed site and embraces the natural landscape. The design is comprised of a glass box flanked by two stone forms, enclosing the garages and transitional space. The glass box is made up of the living room, dining room, and music room and invokes the feeling of floating among the trees while filtered views of the lake trickle through the leaves. A custom steel stairway takes you up to the family retreat or down to the recreation level—and if you explore through the back of the lower level, you might stumble upon a hidden stairway that leads to the subterranean sports court.

FACING PAGE: The fireplace is the center jewel of the living area and the firm had fun mixing stone, steel, and concrete in an elemental way to make it enjoyable from all sides. The corner fire orientation opens it up to both the living room and the entry. In the master bathroom, both the tub and the vanity were placed on windows walls for a flood of light and views into the tree canopies. A two-sided fireplace is shared between the master bedroom and the tub. The master suite is located upstairs, high among the trees, with the rest of the bedrooms just down the hall for an upper-level retreat. Natural stone, reclaimed wood, and warm tones in the beams and finishes complement the green of the surrounding forest that flows in through the windows.
Photographs by Gibeon Photography

"The use of natural materials provides a sense of comfort while uniquely balancing modern living and regional appropriateness."
—Reid Smith

ABOVE: A 10,000-square-foot ski retreat, this home celebrates lightness, sunshine, and color. The south side of the home shows the power of its tremendous number of windows—17-feet-tall walls of glass surround the living and dining rooms—that welcome in year-round sunlight, views and natural light, despite the cold, snowy climate. A large cantilevered, heated patio extends out from underneath the roof eave to enjoy the sunshine while sitting next to the warmth of the gas firepit—or while luxuriating in the custom eight-person stainless-steel hot tub above the patio on the second story. Cantilevered forms and airy elements are also echoed inside, including with the bridge that stretches over to the master wing.

LEFT: A slice through the recreation room's stone backwall allows the wood and steel stairway to wrap around a three-sided, glass-encased wine display. The backlit onyx slab glows at the bottom stair landing providing an interior focal termination while bringing warmth, natural art, and refinement as well as a pop of energy to the lower level.

FACING PAGE TOP: The living room's walls of glass, contrasted with solid stone and wood walls, provide focused panoramic views to the mountainous landscape. Soft wood tones, light, and color bring warmth to the space. A custom concrete mantel and hearth slice the solid wall creating a spot for the fireplace. Motorized artwork slides to the side for TV entertainment.

FACING PAGE BOTTOM LEFT: Floating vanities and mirrors, as seen in this master bathroom, are a theme throughout the house. The privacy glass behind allows natural light to come outside while accommodating views to the outdoors—whenever the homeowners want them.

FACING PAGE BOTTOM RIGHT: High ceilings, large walls of glass, a floating central light fixture, light woods, soft textures, and a slice-through dual-sided fireplace bring warmth, transparency, and brightness to this sun-seeking ski couple's master retreat.
Photographs by Joshua McHugh

BELOW & FACING PAGE: I tend to use water features, patio features, and strategically designed courtyards to create the oasis in the desert that most of my clients are seeking.
Photographs by Deepak Chawla

Richard Luke Architects

Richard Luke Architects, established in Las Vegas in 1986, has come full circle regarding its architectural design. Founder Richard Luke, AIA, moved from Australia to the U.S. in 1984, having been schooled at the Institute of Technology where clean lines and a minimalist aesthetic were encouraged. Now, more than 30 years later, virtually 100 percent of Luke's current designs are modern and contemporary, versus the Mediterranean style that was until recently so popular in Las Vegas.

Luke is widely considered the signature architect for custom residential designs in Las Vegas, having designed homes for founders of some of the world's leading companies, as well as the CEOs of Fortune 100 firms who are mainly referred from elated past clients, all of whom recognize his laser-focus exciting designs, collaborative spirit, friendly demeanor, and attention to detail. Known for plans that are open and spacious, with an emphasis on natural light, Luke is always careful to not block the magnificent views of the Las Vegas Strip—even his covered patios are cantilevered out a minimum of 14 feet. Luke has designed some of the most iconic homes in Las Vegas' most prestigious communities: MacDonald Highlands, The Ridges, The Summit, Queensridge, Seven Hills, Southern Highlands, Lake Las Vegas, and Anthem Country Club.

BELOW: Many of my designs are reminiscent of chic five-star resorts, with indoor-outdoor transitions that are seamless thanks to sliding pocket doors that disappear when they are open and barely-visible thresholds between the floor and the patio.

FACING PAGE: Since I am widely considered the signature architect for custom residential designs in Las Vegas, when people go to sell a house, they say it's a Richard Luke design—it's an advantage in selling a home.
Photographs by JPM Studios

"The pool and landscaping also have to blend and be consistent with the architecture of the house."
—Richard Luke

BELOW & FACING PAGE: It's a challenge to make homes unique while staying within the architectural confines of master-planned communities, but also a gift because it gives me the opportunity to design with many styles, from contemporary to Italianate to Pueblo to Frank Lloyd Wright to modern.
Photographs by Andrew Beneze

"Las Vegas has the best cutting-edge designs and modern architecture happening in the U.S. right now."
—Richard Luke

BELOW & FACING PAGE: The massive windows of this modern Aspen guesthouse reflect its natural surroundings instead of simply imitating them. We carefully laid out the exterior sandstone bands to create a mathematical rhythm echoing the surrounding calm of forest and mountains.
Photographs courtesy of Sinclair Building Architecture Design

Sinclair Building Architecture Design

Sinclair Building Architecture Design is an Aspen-based firm started by Robert G. Sinclair, who brings more than 25 years of experience to the practice. The full- service, multifaceted firm specializes in turnkey design and build for homeowners in Colorado and around the world.

With an appreciation for nature, art, history, and technology, Robert gains a great deal of inspiration through travel. It helps him maintain a flow of creative ideas so that every project is unique. The firm designs in a broad aesthetic range but consistently creates sophisticated homes that are specific to place and time, resulting in a timelessness appeal. The Sinclair team has a saying that every step must be "right, not rushed," which is why every home works so well.

Robert has added a construction division to the firm to gain more control over the outcome of homes. This allows him to work side by side with the homeowner through the entire process and develop a personal relationship with the clients. While embracing modern elements, Robert also holds on to some traditional practices that cannot be replaced—he still draws home designs by hand.

Robert attended the University of Southern California in Los Angeles for his Bachelor of Architecture and went on to earn a master's degree from Syracuse University. He also studied urban design in Florence, Italy. He has received recognition for his work over the years, including state, national, and international design awards.

BELOW & FACING PAGE: Every window offers a complete and sweeping view of the landscape. We created a broad vantage point, with each room enjoying an uninhibited view from Aspen Mountain to Mount Sopris, bookends to the ultimate American alpine panorama.
Photographs courtesy of Sinclair Building Architecture Design

FACING PAGE: The home's new staircase provides an architectural moment, freeing the space from the confines of separated levels and giving the house a focal point. When considering each next element of a project, rather than saying, "Where should we put this?" whether it is an I-beam or a chair, we ask, "Where does this want to be?" Seeing the stairs there now, one cannot imagine them any other way.

BELOW: Part of the beauty of Aspen is that it's a haven of rest, and no space better represents that than a master suite. Completely rearranged, this master bedroom and bathroom found their perfect finishes and fixtures, drawing us into the space, together with tranquility.
Photographs courtesy of Sinclair Building Architecture Design

BELOW: The Orchard House, named for the site's abundant fruit trees, is located just outside Portland's urban growth boundary on former farmland. Our client had just retired and requested a secluded retreat that connected to the landscape while also functioning for entertaining. We were inspired by traditional Japanese "tsuboniwa" courtyard design with the raised walkways surrounding a sculpted landscape.

FACING PAGE: The form of the Orchard House incorporates floating white roof and wall planes separated by glass which slide past each other to create a layered composition.
Photographs by Josh Partee Photography

Steelhead Architecture

"Steelhead" refers both to the building material and to the intrepid fish often associated with the Pacific Northwest—a fitting name for the versatile architecture firm founded in 2010 by Gabriel Headrick, AIA. Steelhead Architecture believes in the sustainable co-existence of the built and natural environments while taking a regional modernist view of architecture that sees the beauty both in our rivers and forests as well as our industrial landscapes.

The firm's wide-ranging experience includes many types of projects—Gabe and his team thrive on variety—from custom modern homes, to multi-family residential, breweries and pubs, mixed-use and commercial work, and beyond. They prioritize green building and high-performance construction, including net zero, Passive House, and LEED rated projects.

As a small creative design firm, Steelhead's clients experience a thoughtful and personal approach, with the firm acting as a guide and friend to navigate the design and construction process. Clients are encouraged to bring ideas to the table and feel comfortable being active participants in the design process. A perfect project is achieving a beautiful, well-conceptualized design while facilitating a creative and enjoyable process and forming lasting relationships.

"The form of the building and the exterior spaces defined and sculpted by the structure are equally important in our design work."
—Gabriel Headrick

ABOVE: The Panavista Hill House is perched on a steep lot in Portland's West Hills. Our design solution for organizing the house and keeping costs in check was to stack the three-story home vertically, with cantilevered volumes in alternating materials for clarity of form and the creation of dynamic outdoor spaces. The majority of the living space is located on the top floor where the site flattens out more and the views to the coast range mountains are the best.

RIGHT: Lightbox 23 Net Zero is a two-unit, certified net zero project in inner northeast Portland. Net zero construction generates as much, or more, energy as is used by the building and is achieved through elements like the 10-kilowatt solar arrays, super insulation, and high-performance mechanical and ventilation systems. The split-level floor plan features floating stairs that act as the central spine, with each floor opening to the half level above and below it

FACING PAGE TOP: From the street, the Orchard House is visible, but partially obscured by the mature fir trees; the meandering driveway reveals more of the house's form upon approach. The large roof overhangs reinforce the horizontal nature of the design and set it into the landscape.

FACING PAGE BOTTOM: The majority of the rooms, including the open-concept living and dining area, are oriented towards the courtyard in the back, reinforcing it as the focal point of the house.
Photographs by Josh Partee Photography

Snow Kreliech Architects, page 281

Morgante–Wilson Architects, page

Mathison | Mathison Architects, page 267

CENTRAL U.S.

BELOW: Because no one can compete with the work of Frank Lloyd Wright, the Thornapple Modern Prairie was intended as a nod to his genius. We designed the home for the homeowners who are avid outdoorspeople, which is why they wanted property along the scenic Thornapple River. In keeping with true Prairie Style, the house was thoughtfully constructed of natural Fond du Lac stone.

FACING PAGE: The eye-catching entrance uses a blend of glass and pivot door, hand-built in Colorado and assembled on site. We used custom-installed cone bearings to make the massive door easy to open. The five-by-seven-foot walnut piece weighs more than 600 pounds.

Photographs by Brian Kelly Photography

42° North - Architecture + Design

Ryan La Haie lives by the idea that if you love what you do, you'll never work a day in your life. It's with that passion that he began 42° North - Architecture + Design, a Michigan-based boutique architecture firm that allows Ryan to practice what he was born to do: design. His grandmother saw a spark early in his childhood and encouraged him to use drawing as an outlet for creativity. Obviously, his grandmother's intuition was correct, as Ryan has spent two decades at some of the most prominent firms in southern Michigan, and eventually became the principal and lead designer at his own firm.

Ryan believes that there is much to be learned from studying the history of architecture and the styles of the past. Carrying that knowledge with him, he and his team utilize today's technology to its fullest extent. Every home is 3-D modeled before breaking ground—this means they can offer the client exterior fly-around videos in addition to interior walk-through videos. The 42° North process is distinct and begins with Ryan spending a day with the homeowners, touring their current house. Clients also complete an in-depth questionnaire that helps convey individual traits and details of their everyday life. Personality and lifestyle become the greatest influencer of the home's design, in addition to the land and surrounding environment. The process continues with planning, schematic design, and design development. Ryan and his team remain engaged the entire time—until the homeowners have their new keys in hand.

BELOW: Our top priority was to maintain river visibility throughout the home and to bring the outdoors in. Just as with the exterior, we used Fond du Lac stone that crosses the threshold of the oversized windows. This allows the natural beauty of the waterfront setting to permeate through the home.

FACING PAGE: The raised, vaulted ceiling in the kitchen features dropped-oak beams to bring warmth to the space, while the sleek vertical-grain oak cabinets emphasize the 10-foot ceilings around the perimeter. We used stacked-transom windows—another feature indicative of Frank Lloyd Wright's Prairie Style. The space has double and steam ovens, dual sinks and dishwashers, and a separate full-size refrigerator and freezer. Here, the marriage of kitchen and screened-in porch creates the ultimate seamless entertainment area with a custom 16-by-9-foot Marvin door that pockets into the wall.
Photographs by Chuck Heiney Photography

ABOVE: The master ensuite features custom-fabricated, dimmable LED backlit mirrors. Inset between the two mirrors is a vertical-grain oak medicine cabinet that is flush with the mirror face. The 180-degree mirrors help reflect light, as well as make the space feel large and bright. Wall-mounted faucets allow for a clean and uninterrupted quartz countertop while taking up less space. The marble floors extend upwards towards the ceiling, creating a sleek and cohesive aesthetic.

CENTER: Dimensional gloss-black wall tiles complement the Calacatta marble and contrast the warmth of the solid oak entry door. The shower features an integrated cantilever ceramic bench and a linear floor drain. The shower walls and ceiling utilize large ceramic tile sheets to create a continuous appearance while minimizing grout lines.

BELOW: The house was meticulously positioned on the site to encapsulate three distinct views of the river beyond. The front of the house was splayed to maximize the use of the site, allowing the courtyard entry to the garage. A garage-over-garage construction provides a shop for the homeowners, with a private access stairway. The main level of the home was designed for a seamless aging-in-place experience. A screened porch can be either separate or act as an extension of the kitchen with large disappearing glass doors. This lends itself to entertaining large groups and makes for the ultimate indoor-outdoor living experience.

FACING PAGE: We designed the home for empty nesters who wanted a modern spin on the traditional Prairie-Style home. The result is a beautiful combination of form and function, with special attention paid to detail in both architecture and design. We created the entryway to make the home's first dramatic statement. The flush exterior walkway leads to a five-by-seven walnut pivot door with a glass surround. This eye-catching door is encompassed by chocolate-brown Norman brick. Horizontal siding is purposefully staggered to draw the eye toward the impressive entry.
Photographs by Chuck Heiney Photography

"The greatest compliment I've received is, 'Wow, your work is very diverse.' I try to pay homage to any true architectural style."
—Ryan La Haie

"A well-designed home harnesses natural light, which is imperative to our well-being and health."
—Ryan La Haie

ABOVE: We designed the Mountain Modern Residence for a family of four who loves being outdoors. It sits atop a steep hill on a 40-acre natural site with views of the sky-lined treetops. The home is steel framed and features exposed steel beams that extend from the interior to the exterior.

CENTER: Waterfront Modern sits on a private cul-de-sac and was created for a recreation-loving family. It features a golf simulator and a waterfall-edge pool that overlooks the lake at the rear of the home.

BOTTOM: We captured the spirt of the Frank Lloyd Wright Usonian house with Modern Serenity. It has a low, linear profile accompanied by expansive windows. The living space opens up to a large lanai overlooking the serene river.

FACING PAGE: The horizontal design used on the exterior continues inside with a rich walnut wall that runs parallel to the dark hardwood flooring. The hallway was lined with warm walnut that spans the length of the home. The open floor plan is flooded with natural light streaming in from the glass back wall. In the kitchen, we created visual interest by using oak lower cabinets paired with glossy white upper cabinets. The entire space is a study in balance and symmetry. Tucked around the corner is a generous walk-in pantry designed as a catch-all, keeping the main kitchen clean, sleek, and clutter free.
Photographs by Ashley Avila Photography
Renderings by Sean Tracey, Tracey Illustration

BELOW & FACING PAGE: This sinuous, lake-front home's light, floating roofs are anchored to its site by heavy rusticated limestone masses, while its horizontal footprint is spread out and sewn through a vertical foreground of mature sycamore, cypress, and pecan trees. Tooled limestone walls invoke a sense of history and permanence in character with the surroundings and offer a counterpoint to the transparency of the home's public spaces.
Photographs by Casey Dunn

A Parallel Architecture

Partners Eric Barth and Ryan Burke believe that design is primarily a tool for solving problems, not adding complexity. As much a process of editing as it is one of creating, this philosophical framework is the basis for their work. This approach is rigorously applied to all aspects of their projects and yields a consistent emphasis on site responsiveness and meaningful innovation.

Barth and Burke understand that buildings are beholden to their site, whether physically, climatically, or contextually. Each site offers unique opportunities and constraints, and designing within these parameters instills a building with appropriateness. The firm plays a lead role in all design aspects of a project, including interiors and landscape design, in order to create a cohesive and unified vision for the project.

A Parallel Architecture embraces every project as an opportunity to collaborate and create, working in concert with client, consultant, and contractor to form an inspired team with parallel objectives and a common goal. Their team relies heavily on immersive 3-D design—which includes detailed modeling, virtual reality, and photorealistic renderings—in order to ensure a project's parameters are thoroughly understood, vetted, and conveyed before substantial resources are committed to building it.

FACING PAGE & BELOW: Expansive glass and oversized pocketing, sliding doors extend the livable footprint of the home to the outdoors and capitalize on the scenic lakefront. A warm interior palette of oak, mahogany, and cedar serves as a soft counterpoint to the glass and stone, exuding a relaxed livability. At the glassy center of the home, the structural system is exposed to reveal a rhythmic steel vertebrate that organizes the primary public spaces and provides definition and scale to the spacious rooms. *Photographs by Casey Dunn*

BELOW: Clean lines and a mixture of textures and materials define the simple façade of this house that sits on a sloped lot, taking full advantage of the downtown Austin city view. On the exterior, we played with different local materials, creating color and texture contrast with local wood, local limestone, and stucco for a contemporary mood. The home looks deceptively small from the front, offering a surprise to everyone who opens the front door to see the full expanse of the split-level property which grows downward.

FACING PAGE: Open floor plans, high ceilings, and beautiful views create a wow factor in this kitchen and living area.
Photographs by Mark Adams

AHS Design Group

Luciana Corwin has always been fascinated with residential design; even as a child, her favorite pastime was visiting open houses and interpreting the layouts and floor plans.

Now, as founder and principal of AHS Design Group, she takes her innate eye for design to create dynamic environments that impact people's feelings and mood. Together with the team at AHS, she works on architecture and interior design for residential and small commercial projects in the Austin, Texas area. However, her extensive world travels as well as previously living in four different countries has allowed her to bring a diverse, global perspective and innovative solutions to her clients.

What's most important to AHS, though, is collaboration with owners; it is key to their process in order to achieve customized, purpose-driven spaces that make sense. The firm also prioritizes the relation between shape, volume, texture, and color to create a beautiful harmony of design that is unique to each project.

BELOW TOP: This North Austin house has an open floor plan with an industrial feel, achieved through the use of steel, exposed ducts, and exposed brick—with some wood touches to warm the environment.

BELOW BOTTOM LEFT: The exterior evokes modern simplicity with contrasting wood and stucco.

BELOW BOTTOM RIGHT: The open floor plan features rooms that face out to an intimate courtyard.
Photographs by Mark Adams

BELOW TOP: The easy comfort and sophistication of this home in Central Austin is punctuated by exposed ductwork to riff on elegant industrialism.

BELOW BOTTOM: The industrial-modern staircase, with its warm woods and simple lines, echoes the clean yet cozy aesthetic of the living room it overlooks. The room faces an intimate courtyard.
Photographs by Mark Adams

"We are not just creating spaces, but a whole environment that plays with how people feel."
—Luciana Corwin

BELOW TOP: These tree houses form their own village in the Austin area. With a nod to simplicity and a few changes in exterior materials to create a wooden slat effect, we brought this "barn-style" house to the city.

BELOW BOTTOM LEFT: Inside, the barn-style house goes sleek with streamlined textures in the cabinets, polished backsplash, stainless appliances, and wood plank floors.
Photographs by Twist Tours

BELOW TOP: We wanted this unique take on a floating staircase to offer a sculptural element, punctuating the easy comfort and elegance of the home.

BELOW BOTTOM: The exterior of this contemporary home in the fun, hipster area of East Austin boasts hues of soft gray, warm brown, and bold red to create an eye-catching color palette. Concrete pavers define the walkway to the front porch area.
Photographs by Jayme Ivison

"The experiential aspect of design is what I find most fascinating."
—Luciana Corwin

BELOW & FACING PAGE: Located on a six-acre wooded property overlooking a wetland and lake beyond, this home was designed to celebrate the natural beauty and views of the property. The couple wanted it to exist as a reflection of stewardship of the land. The design of the "shiny shed" seeks to be a counterpoint to the house that dissolves into the site through fractured reflections. Mirrored stainless steel panels of varying angles reflect and animate the views of the surrounding woods.
Photographs by Paul Crosby

ALTUS Architecture + Design

Light is the creator of architecture, believes Timothy A. Alt, the founder and principal of ALTUS Architecture + Design. How light is captured in various spaces throughout a home or what qualities it displays at different times of day are both vital considerations that Alt and his team respect when starting a new project. Being conscious of a home's site—and building with, rather than against, its natural properties—is the foundation of ALTUS's design philosophy, which Alt has distinguished as "organic minimalism." He describes it as a distilled reflection of the site and integration of the living environment, as well as building with materials and craftsmanship that reflect a timeless, natural architecture that unifies the projects within the setting.

Though Alt considers organic minimalism the guiding principle for his full-service architecture and interior design firm, he is careful to avoid prescribing other "signatures" in his designs. With advancing technology and emerging green design both playing a role in this era, it's important to understand the qualities and issues present in all great architecture over time. Only then can each project be truly unique.

BELOW: The design expression reflects "organic minimalism" through a distilled composition of wood, glass, and stone. The structural frame of cedar and infill panels of vertical cedar siding are stained a dark translucent grey to complement the bark of the surrounding trees. Glass between the structural frame creates transparency to the natural surroundings. A bluestone base, fireplace, flooring, and terrace connect the house to the site. The organic quality of the materials was chosen to honor the site and convey a quiet belonging on the property.
Photographs by Paul Crosby

BELOW: The white walls and walnut panels create a sculptural form within the tall volume in the middle of the property. Floor-to-ceiling windows provide dramatic views and blur the line between inside and outside, while the walnut and bluestone floors, walnut cabinetry, and white walls for displaying art create a tactile and crisp interior as a complement to the organic beauty of the site. A prefabricated cedar pergola and steel trellis create shade for the interior spaces, while also serving as an outdoor room overlooking the wetland beyond.
Photographs by Paul Crosby

"In this period of maturing Modernism, advancing technology, and emerging green design, one must understand the qualities and issues present in all great architecture over time."
—Timothy Alt

217

BELOW: A sculptural response to the oak trees and lake, the design of this industrial modern house for a family of eight in Waconia, Minnesota, promotes their active lifestyle. An indoor swimming pool creates togetherness through the seasons.

FACING PAGE: The exterior materials fold into the house over a concrete floor as an "indestructible" palette, integrating indoor and outdoor living. A steel and concrete bridge links the bedroom wings. Natural and colored plywood walls animate the lofted bedrooms in the children's wing.
Photographs by Paul Crosby

"The qualities and character that your home conveys reflect your personal values and way of living."
—Timothy Alt

BELOW: The home's design celebrates its surroundings through natural materials and transparency.

FACING PAGE: The living room "void" volume of glass separates the upper level bedroom wings.
Photographs by Paul Crosby

BELOW: The owners' dream was a residential retreat that would allow them to "follow the sun" throughout the day and the seasons, with the various living spaces oriented to the natural light. This was the last open site on the rim of the Nichols Arboretum, so it was especially challenging to design this home in dialogue with the landscape while considering the topography, views, orientation, and materials. Baked ash exterior siding not only contrasts with the stucco; the vertical panels reference the tree trunks to echo the surrounding woodland.

FACING PAGE: The rear view of the home allows a peek into the master bedroom suite on the second floor with the main living spaces below. Generous windows provide views into the Arboretum and the vertical baked ash siding contrasts with the horizontal lines of the stucco and windows. The siding is installed horizontally at the rear of the courtyard to bridge and unify the two wings of the home.
Photographs by Jeff Garland

Angelini & Associates Architects

Angelini & Associates Architects founders Brad Angelini and Theresa Angelini work together and share in influencing the design of every project—along with their talented team of eight other architects and architectural designers. The firm offers a scholarly approach to developing comprehensive architectural solutions while providing design services, programming, and master planning for a wide variety of building types. Each project is shaped by careful consideration of the client's needs and desires as well as site influences, exterior materials, interior finishes, structure, lighting, and budgets.

While every project has a specific team dedicated to it, the open and lively communication within the Angelini & Associates office means that the entire firm always shares insights and experiences to benefit each project. The Angelinis also believe that their collaborative process works the best when all key stakeholders are meaningfully involved every step of the way—and that includes the homeowners, architect, consultants, and builder.

Indeed, for the Angelinis, the homeowner is highly integral to the design; it's a priority they have held since they launched their practice in 1989. They know that the most rewarding projects are those in which the clients know they've had an important influence in the design; it's this listening, collaboration, and synergy that breathes life into every residence.

BELOW TOP: The west open courtyard is nestled into the wings of the house, extending the main living and dining spaces to the outdoors and capitalizing on the views. The private deck from the master suite den above the dining room provides secluded outdoor space with a bird's eye view into the Arboretum. Large windows wrapping the corners extend the space diagonally through the rooms. The ledgestone fireplace chimney provides vertical emphasis and contrast with the smooth stucco finish and horizontal window lines.

BELOW BOTTOM: The house's H-shaped plan is anchored by a stair tower and elevator, so that the massing of the house steps up the hill and then strategically opens towards the Arboretum. Sunlight is celebrated during the day, but at night, the mood is just as warm with ambient lighting throughout the home and landscape.
Photographs by Jeff Garland

"Our goal is to create residences that are simultaneously intentional and effortless; homes that converse with their surroundings and speak to their homeowners in a powerfully personal way."
—Brad Angelini

BELOW TOP: The kitchen anchors both the living room and dining room as the heart of the home for entertaining and cooking. The island is the focus for conversational gathering at one end with functional space for two cooks on the other sides. A discreetly located pantry houses small appliances and messier items to keep the counters free of clutter.

BELOW BOTTOM LEFT: The flat roofs of the guest wing and garage allow the main living spaces to rise above them, taking full advantage of the light and views. The wood storage for the high-efficiency fireplace is built into the south side of the garage, making the logs a beautifully integrated and convenient feature.

BELOW BOTTOM RIGHT: The retreat-like master bedroom suite den and private upper deck overlook the open courtyard and the Arboretum beyond. Horizontal siding and guardrails unify the wings of the home while horizontal fencing provides privacy toward the neighbor's home and conceals the roof access.
Photographs by Jeff Garland

225

FACING PAGE: This home is carefully sited at the opening of a wooded ravine where one of the homeowners played as a child. The two major living spaces—the living room on the upper level and the family room on the lower level—are oriented with a focused view to the ravine through a two-story window wall. The two-sided fireplace likewise creates a dialogue between the inside and out; it faces the living room on one side and the glass window wall on the other. The exterior deck cantilevers toward the ravine, providing another opportunity to experience the view—this time, as if on the prow of a ship.

BELOW TOP: The kitchen offers a central anchoring point with a generous island, cooking, and desk area. White walls provide the backdrop for bold orange and blue accents.

BELOW BOTTOM: The living room, dining room, and kitchen open to each other and are unified by the wood-clad open ceiling space. Colorful artwork and furnishings reinforce a joyful, radiant vibe in the home.
Photographs by Jeff Garland

"A collage of windows artistically frames the view and sets a theatrical stage to connect the indoors with the outside."
—Theresa Angelini

BELOW & FACING PAGE: Located at the bend of a meandering river, the Rock River House respects as it reflects its surroundings. Our design objective was to create a functional and efficient home with panoramic views of the glistening water below and the forested nature preserve beyond. The house is assembled from a collection of stepping volumes that recall the nearby crescent-shaped, waterfall edge.
Photographs by Tricia Shay Photography

Bruns Architecture

Stephen Bruns founded his namesake firm in 2008 with a passion for architecture and a simple goal: to create pure, meaningful designs that are translated into well crafted structures. Bruns Architecture specializes in highly detailed residential and commercial environments. It offers a full range of architectural and design services to manage a project from initial concept and planning through final detailing, construction administration, and furniture design.

Stephen and his team's comprehensive approach begins with a process of discovery. They listen to the client and investigate the site, carefully researching to understand the influences of a project. Through careful composition, selective materiality, strong connection to the site, and in specific response to program and budget, the team offers a consistent vision and the value of good design. One of the primary core values is sustainability. Whether the homeowner's goals are to have a LEED certified project, or simply to reduce operating expenses through more efficient and technologically advanced building systems, Bruns Architecture can help achieve the objective.

Stephen's carefully crafted solutions have received numerous awards, including AIA Wisconsin Honor Awards and ALA Design Awards. Stephen was also the recipient of the Richard M. Raemer Memorial Award and the LaSalle Partners Fellowship in Architecture.

BELOW TOP & BOTTOM: With two distinct personalities, the composition modulates its apparent scale. From the street, the construct fits amicably into the modest fabric of the neighborhood as a series of furniture-like wood boxes. It then unfolds into a transparent lens affording uninterrupted views to the water beyond. Wall and ceiling planes are arranged carefully to display kaleidoscopic reflections of sunlight off the water.

FACING PAGE TOP & BOTTOM: The glazing is specifically engineered to reflect winter heat inward while rejecting summer solar gain. It also maximizes visible light transmittance for optimal views to nature. Stone from a neighboring Wisconsin quarry passes through the glass wall, blurring the distinction between interior and exterior spaces.
Photographs by Tricia Shay Photography

"We distill the essence of every project. The resulting vision becomes an invaluable tool that guides the design process. We believe our holistic approach is what sets us apart."
—Stephen Bruns

231

BELOW: Set within the diverse landscape of the University of Wisconsin Arboretum neighborhood, Arboretum House grows out of its forested site as a cultivated collection of forms that combine to create an architectural ecosystem. Our design objective was to create a home with minimal impact on the existing vegetation. Precisely extended roof eaves work in concert with the house's orientation to utilize the foliage of the surrounding deciduous trees as a natural shading element in the warm summer months. Cross ventilation through carefully placed, operable windows eliminates the need for air conditioning.

FACING PAGE TOP & CENTER: We used precise studies of the existing trees and topography to inform the placement, site, and organization of the house. Portions of the structure cantilever into the site, reducing the footprint and reflecting the dense tree canopies above. At the entry, a floating wood canopy provides shelter as it extends deep into the interior, drawing one's view through the house to the woodland beyond.

FACING PAGE BOTTOM: Five trees from the home's footprint were harvested, dried, and milled to become ceilings, soffits, and stairs—the felled timber of this cherished site will forever be experienced and enjoyed.
Photographs by Tricia Shay Photography

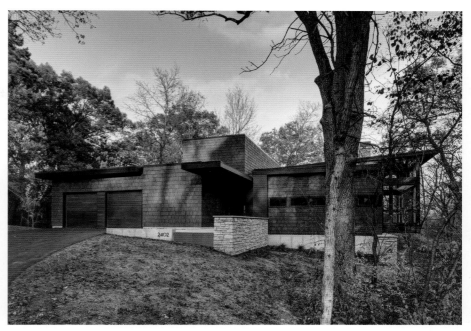

BELOW & FACING PAGE: A past client was ready to make some accessibility updates to their 100-plus-year-old farmhouse that had recently been modernized. The desire was a simple age-in-place concept that would better integrate with their healthy lifestyle, connection with the outdoors, and their impressive modern art and furniture collection. Melissa and the director of residential design, Jason Ekstrom, quickly realized the disparity between the outdated envelope needing costly renovations and the dream home that would meet the clients' desires. Rather than end the design process, the client elected to have our team create a new home that truly represented their goals. The result is a clean, modern space with a warm, comfortable atmosphere.
Photographs by Tricia Shay Architectural Photography

Destree Design Architects, Inc.

Melissa Destree founded her namesake firm in 2000, concentrating on planning, architecture, and interior design. Destree Design Architects has grown into a collaborative company that focuses on personalized service and elegant buildings. With Destree Design, the client is an integral part of the team and their opinions, suggestions, and concerns are heard with an open mind and creative spirit. The firm is committed to environmental responsibility, energy efficiency, and alternate energy solutions, and always considers the site's specific challenges and virtues. The team strives to educate their clients and give them the tools they need to be good stewards to the earth's natural resources.

Destree Design team creates interiors and buildings that range from single and multi-family residences to corporate, hospitality, retail, and municipal projects. With a varied base of architectural and interior design expertise, this woman-owned firm also provides consulting services, facility studies, space programming, branding implementation, code evaluations, furniture coordination, and construction administration services. They believe creativity flourishes and designs are quickly refined when different perspectives and design options are considered. Teamwork is essential to successful design.

ABOVE & LEFT: Three ideas informed Ekstrom's design vision for this Nordic modern home: solidity, simplicity, and grace. Solidity is expressed in the steel beams, concrete, and bold, black exterior. Simplicity is seen in the clean lines, neutral palette, and visible structural features. Finally, grace is exhibited in its harmony with the surrounding restored Oak savannah. It is exemplified in the continuity of the wood-clad ceiling from interior to exterior spaces, the abundance of windows, and the weightlessness of the cantilevered staircase.

FACING PAGE: The concrete and wood beams of the entry create strong lines that are contrasted by the openness of the wood-slatted surround and the light and shadows that play within throughout the day.
Photographs by Tricia Shay Architectural Photography

ABOVE & LEFT: To personalize the design for our clients, a structural engineer and an executive, all the interior finishes were selected to highlight the steel and concrete. Third-grade white maple floors brighten the space, while the blackness of the sap accentuates the exposed structural materials. Gallery-style lighting illuminates the artwork throughout the home. All the existing furniture was integrated into the design, including two concrete lounge chairs that command attention at the base of the stair. These chairs were discovered at a local gallery and originally intended for the client's office, but were a seamless addition to the home aesthetic.

FACING PAGE: Metal is the star of the great room. A steel hearth and wall element surround the pivoting fireplace and an adjoining steel shelf stores firewood and displays art. The kitchen island counter exhibits a single plate of quarter-inch steel, bending in a graceful fold to the maple floors. Steel is repeated in the stove backsplash while glass mosaic at the sink creates texture and captures light.
Photographs by Tricia Shay Architectural Photography

"The design process is an incredible thing, a true journey. It is even more incredible when it takes you down a path that is entirely unexpected."
—Melissa Destree

BELOW & FACING PAGE: The four-bedroom home sits on a five-acre site in semi-rural Racine, Wisconsin, clad in red brick and cedar siding. It takes inspiration from Palladio's Villa Rotunda in Vicenza, Italy, which was based on the classic 9-square planning system. The Villa Rotunda has a raised center portion with a dome above as its main point of spatial drama.
Photographs by Kenneth Dahlin

Genesis Architecture LLC

Kenneth Dahlin came across the work of Frank Lloyd Wright in a library book when he was just 14, and was immediately inspired by the beauty and sense of nature he saw in the legend's designs. He founded Genesis Architecture in 1992 with the aim of creating his own organic and compelling buildings in the vein of Wright, producing architecture that resonates with the human soul as well as with nature.

Today, Dahlin is known for his specialization in Wrightian/organic design but he also embraces the challenge of blending the desires of the homeowner with the cues of the landscape. Creating a symphony of brick, wood, and stone, which will inspire the inhabitants for years to come, is always the aim. Knowing that materials and styles can be remodeled later but a house's bones are much harder to change, Dahlin urges his clients to put the focus on the timeless design principles of harmony, beauty, creativity, and context while bringing their residences into the 21st century. A good sense of space and light is vital, but nothing tops the satisfaction of living in a work of art that enhances and inspires life.

BELOW TOP: The central vertical space is capped with a glass pyramid rather than a dome. The light from the skylight trickles down into the upstairs loft, which is suspended between the adjoining walls and creates a gap where that light can reflect indirectly down into the living room.

BELOW BOTTOM: The kitchen is outfitted with Sub-Zero and Wolf appliances and custom concrete countertops. A breakfast area with south-facing glass opens out to a landscaped patio area with built-in grill.
Photographs by Kenneth Dahlin

BELOW: The master suite is on the highest level and has its own reading loft under the pyramid skylight. This loft is accessed by a few steps that rise up between two masonry piers which are an extension of the fireplace chase. At the top of this short flight of steps is a glass bridge that connects to the "floating" reading loft, which from the living room below looks like a suspended wood cube hovering above with light washing down the sides of it.
Photographs by Kenneth Dahlin

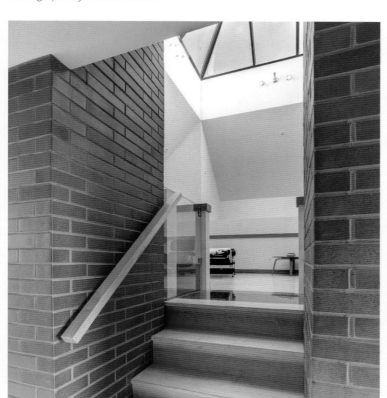

"When done well, there is a poetry to architecture that achieves harmony with nature."
—Kenneth Dahlin

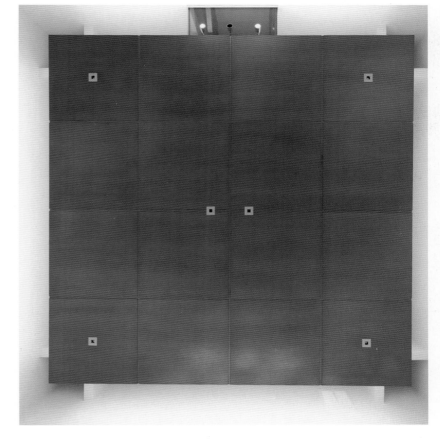

BELOW & FACING PAGE: When we designed a modern home that has three public sides—two street-facing and one toward a golf course—the main challenge was creating privacy for the homeowners. The first thing we did was to conduct a tree survey to preserve and utilize as many of the mature trees as possible, since they provide lush, natural cover. For the pool and outdoor living space, it was imperative that it remain hidden from the golf course, so we designed a long, linear stone wall that complements the architecture, but maintains the owners' privacy.
Photographs by Ryan Woodall

Goldberg Design Group

For more than 30 years, Goldberg Design Group has been a leader in residential architecture in Indiana. Located in Carmel, the firm was started by Stephen B. Goldberg who has had a passion for architecture since his elementary school days. His family moved frequently so he got quite a few chances to tour homes and see a variety of regional styles and floor plans. He began sketching plans at age seven based on these experiences, and later starting collecting blueprints to examine how those professionals communicated their designs. It only made sense then that Stephen began designing and building impressive custom homes even before graduating with his degree in architecture from St. Louis' Washington University.

In recent years, Indiana has seen an influx of residents, drawn by the state's great schools, low cost of living, and traditional values. With that has come a wide range of interest in home styles and Goldberg Design Group has happily accommodated nearly all of them. The team has designed everything from lakefront cottages to ultra-modern estates, and worked across the country, including Florida, Tennessee, and Illinois. They've also designed homes in far-off locations such as Tanzania and Turks and Caicos. The firm has received recognition, including an AIA local chapter award for Best Residential Design and inclusion on the Top 100 Luxury Residential Architecture Firms in Northern America by Bond Custom, an international forum representing leaders of global architecture and design.

BELOW TOP: Set in the historic village of Zionsville, this home is nestled into a plot of land that is a little more than one acre. Even though its style is different than surrounding designs, the home works because it blends into the site so well.

BELOW BOTTOM: When a homeowner wanted cool colors for a contemporary interior, I chose shades of white and gray, and used sleek, eye-catching chandeliers to bring the room together.
Photographs by Stephen Goldberg

"I'm not committed to one single look. I can capture any period or style of home with equal finesse—but modern is my personal favorite."
—Stephen B. Goldberg

BELOW: Our firm was honored when we were chosen to design the Indianapolis Monthly Dream Home, for the fourth time—a prestigious annual award given out by the magazine. The estate sits on a little more than 50 acres of land and features an exterior of rich brown simulated wood and smooth limestone cladding. It boasts a metal roof, six-car garage, porte cochere, and approximately 13,000 square feet of finished living area. We collaborated with a talented landscape architect who created the luxurious half-million-dollar swimming pool and fire features.
Photographs by Mark Bradley

BELOW & FACING PAGE: This 1968 home was purchased by a young client eager to push the design envelope. Our principal objective was finding a playful way to embrace the original bones of the house while incorporating modern luxuries and unwrapping the home to the outdoors. The connection with the outdoors is reinforced with the large sweeping roofs that morph into a "Cadillac fin" shed, adding a third vertical dimension by way of an aperture to the sky.
Photographs by Leonid Furmansky

John Grable Architects

John Grable's architecture celebrates life. By connecting to history and expressing a deep love of craft and material, his work articulates purity and simplicity, and exalts the relationship between man and nature. A passion for the stories of people's lives and the role of buildings in them drives Grable's design. By building on existing traditions and historic vernacular, his work not only contributes to the continuum of the human experience but also keeps the history of a place alive and evolving.

Coming full circle and connecting physically to what came before, Grable feels an obligation to reuse and recycle materials. His work is enlivened by a creative blend of old materials often playfully adapted to new applications. By embracing time-tested building techniques that complement nature and taking care to rehabilitate materials whenever possible, his work is a joyous convergence of past and present. He is co-founder of and former teacher at the LakelFlato Graduate Design Studio at the University of Texas San Antonio and has lectured and served on design juries throughout the country. Grable is also an inspiring teacher and mentor. With a tenured and fully licensed staff all under 40, he has spawned a new generation of young architects who consult with clients and mentor the trade on a daily basis.

"We are students of history—if we weren't, we'd all be out there trying to reinvent the wheel."
—John Grable, FAIA

RIGHT & FACING PAGE: The existing double-width brick walls that operated as bookends inspired a newly expansive "warehouse" space in the form of a barbell—a form bounded on the ends and open in the middle, known and revered in Texas as a Dog Run. The introduction of an infinity-edge pool to the existing entry courtyard harks back to the traditional regional roots of the acequias that were a part of the original hacienda courtyard entries. Large expanses of glass allow the great room's spacious volumes to leak out in every direction.
Photographs by Leonid Furmansky

251

"The best interior designer is Mother Nature."
—John Grable, FAIA

ABOVE & RIGHT: The main entry bridge enlivens these outdoor spaces with a grotto waterfall niche that complements the cool shade of the heritage trees that reside throughout the yard. Additionally, wall-to-wall sliding doors in the living area open up to expand the room out into the pool and landscape that provides additional outdoor space for entertaining.

FACING PAGE: Sited on a corner lot of the Alamo Heights neighborhood, overlooking the Olmos Basin with views of downtown and their beloved alma mater, this innovative single-family residence was built upon the architect and client's mutual respect for the environment. With the foundation of sustainability as a responsible and moral obligation of built form, the challenge was to balance innovative sustainable technologies with time-honored techniques while also drawing from and integrating with the historic context of the neighborhood.
Photographs by Dror Baldinger, FAIA

BELOW & FACING PAGE: Bounded by a verdant nature trail, this corner lot utilizes a modern "one room wide" open plan—consistent with historical precedence—that mimics the proportions of the original neighborhood cottages. Exterior steel arbors serve as protection from the sun, casting ever-changing shadows on the white stucco walls. Housed in the traditional bay window stairwell, the open, hanging, folded, and blackened finish steel plate stair subtly emphasizes the materiality while melding with the black painted steel structure throughout, delivering unobstructed courtyard views. This home and its design solutions are the epitome of a small site with big living.
Photographs by Dror Baldinger, FAIA

BELOW & FACING PAGE: Sited directly off the creek banks of a tributary to the Guadalupe River, this floating structure was erected to serve as a sanctuary for both music and health. The dual corner windows, flanking a steel column, bathe early morning light upon the baby grand piano, which is bounded by the two cypress walls. The project was sited within the floodplain and floats above the land on oil rig steel pipe pilotes, as homage to five generations of the family legacy within the oil industry.
Photographs by John Grable Architects

"You can advance your thought process just by studying the past."

—John Grable, FAIA

BELOW & FACING PAGE: We designed the Sumner Bohannon House for a site that required careful preservation of the slope and trees. Adjacent to a 100-year floodplain, the home had to be carefully integrated into the site's considerable natural grade, protecting the surrounding mature trees. The distinctive exterior is clad in painted brick accented with vertical cedar screens shielding walls and certain large expanses of windows. Galvanized metal is utilized for roofing and exterior wall cladding, particularly where the roof and wall planes intersect. Large areas of glass, oriented to the views, make up the final exterior element.
Photographs by Dror Baldinger, FAIA Photography

Malone Maxwell Borson Architects

For Michael Malone, FAIA founding principal of Malone Maxwell Borson Architects, popular design trends are overrated as design inspiration. The firm's work emphasizes responding to the unique aspects of the site and understanding the homeowner's lifestyle. These components matter in the long run and contribute to how the house is used and enjoyed. Often countering the media's presentation of fads and visual cues, Malone Maxwell Borson creates homes that strive for timelessness, eschewing a particular style. The team finds this philosophy refreshing and fun—and an expanding list of enthusiastic clients agree. It embodies the idea that the client-architect experience should result in a unique and personal expression, best suiting the client's aspirations.

Founded in 1992, Malone Maxwell Borson Architects is a full-service architectural firm designing commercial, corporate, religious, educational, and co-working spaces in addition to the flagship residential portfolio. Michael finds his inspiration from the visual world—everything around him is the basis for ideas. Through close observation, you'll experience a vast variety of patterns, variations, and forms to draw from in art, nature, and everyday surroundings. Frequent travel also generates inspiration, recorded by Michael in drawings and sketches. These are also tools for working out problems and exploring design solutions. You can find Malone Maxwell Borson Architects' residential and commercial work in 31 states and most major cities. At home, the Dallas Chapter of the American Institute of Architects recognized the firm as the Architecture Firm of the Year in 2013.

BELOW: Freestanding architectural elements serve as partitions in the spacious living area, dividing a dining room and the upper- and lower-level living rooms. These spaces are unified under an undulating ceiling mimicking the site's slope and focusing views to the exterior and scenic creek beyond. A fireplace separates the dining area from the living room, and a large console acts as a divider between the upper and lower level. We designed a sculptural steel and wood stair to provide vertical circulation and act as a hinge between the public and private spaces of the home. The master bedroom is on the lower floor and two children's bedrooms and a play area are on the upper.

FACING PAGE: To simplify the interior and emphasize the views, we edited the material palette to a few selections for the entire house. Large format terra cotta flooring is used consistently, unifying the ground level and mitigating glare from the many windows. Generous use of maple warms the indoor spaces and forms the basis for a variety of design elements: millwork, paneling, and as the undulating ceiling plane of the living room.

Photographs by Dror Baldinger, FAIA Photography

"It's hard to pin down exactly what makes a room enjoyable, but I believe that scale and orientation—combined with some access to natural light—are the most important elements of any residential space."
—Michael Malone, FAIA

261

BELOW & FACING PAGE:: The Hart Woodson House sits on more than an acre, high on a clifftop above Lake Austin. To the west is the view of the lake, which isn't ideal for solar orientation. Naturally, the homeowner wanted the house to face the water, but with intense Texas heat, the direct sun exposure was a challenge that had to be addressed. The largest living space is oriented east-west with only one narrow, west-facing exposure. A retractable shade is automatically activated by a sensor that tracks the sun's movement across the sky, adjusting the shade in response to the amount of direct solar heat gain.
Photographs by Dror Baldinger, FAIA Photography

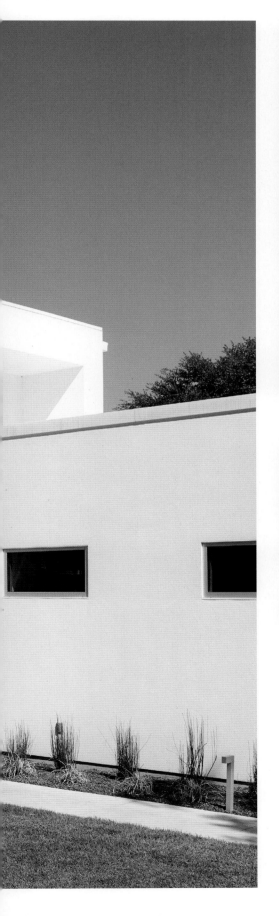

"No two sites are the same, no two sets of expectations, and no two outcomes. Finding a way to solve a design problem, in a new and interesting way, is always satisfying."
—Michael Malone, FAIA

"We prefer a sense of openness, large expanses of glass, warm materials like wood and stone, and careful detailing."
—Michael Malone, FAIA

BELOW & FACING PAGE: We designed the home with casual entertaining in mind—for both the indoor and the outdoor spaces. A large kitchen provides easy access to the dining room and the playroom, which open into the living room and extend the indoor spaces into the landscape. The large west window overlooks the pool and the hills beyond. It's an ideal spot to catch a Hill Country sunset. The high ceilings and glass walls bring the outdoors in.
Photographs by Dror Baldinger, FAIA Photography

BELOW: Riverglass is inspired by the transparent reflections captured in the unique setting on the Thornapple River that features a 200-degree water view. The entry makes a dramatic statement with its sculptural three-story atrium that separates the public and private spaces of the home. The exterior's Western red cedar lends warmth to the 6,300 square-foot dwelling while expansive glass offers up a constant conversation with nature.

FACING PAGE: We thought about this house as a threshold to the river whereby the architecture unfolds gradually into the landscape, providing a continuous experience from the inside to the outside. A deep overhang creates a transitional resting place for the outdoor patio area.
Photographs by Jason Keen

Mathison | Mathison Architects

Mathison | Mathison Architects (MMA) creates meaningful spaces with a modern aesthetic. Founded on the conviction that architecture, planning, and design elevate lives, co-principals Tom Mathison and Evan Mathison, along with their talented team of architects and designers, discover new opportunities to raise the function, comfort, and sustainability of every structure they design.

MMA's ultimate mission is to create places that respond thoughtfully to the needs of their clients and the environment. They use the interplay of light, material, and texture in a holistic and informed design approach to yield functional and sustainable results. Indeed, their integration of sustainable strategies and their understanding of alternative construction delivery methods result in high levels of environmental and financial responsibility.

Rigorous planning and creative design drive MMA's process and execution while their collaborative style encourages deeper discussion, innovative perspectives, and fresh insight. It also fosters an environment of partnership towards a common goal, emphasizing client engagement as a critical and integral part of the team.

"Exceptional design connects people with space and with each other."
—Evan Mathison

ABOVE: As the highest point of the house, the third floor provides multi-directional views and is reserved for focused work, reflection, wellness, and inspiration. While there is visibility to the upper floors through the glass and slat walls, the distance between the public and private levels provides a clear distinction and division of space.

RIGHT: Glass bridges connect the private upper floors while maintaining the open and naturally lit aesthetic of the home.

FACING PAGE TOP: Across the interior, the modern architecture is complemented with tailored furniture in classic finishes that evoke warmth and comfort. In the open living room, the scale is low and grounded to draw attention to the high ceilings and prominent exterior river views, which serve as the focal point for the space.

FACING PAGE BOTTOM: The interior of the home echoes its modernity of form, adding a layer of softness to the precise edges through the warmth of wood paneling and a fire feature.
Photographs by Jason Keen

"Structure, space, and connection between interior and exterior are essential to creating a meaningful home that is elegant and balanced—regardless of its size or complexity."
—Tom Mathison

BELOW: A multi-generational family lives in the Hudson Valley House and they invite visitors to enjoy the property year-round. Five equal-size bedrooms and shared bathrooms express a democratic set of values, allowing a higher level of attention to the indoor and outdoor shared areas, including the main living room. Natural wood slats and expansive windows blur the line between the interior and exterior.

FACING PAGE TOP: The cantilevered form of the Hudson Valley House gives the feeling of floating over the landscape as it protects guests from the elements in the outdoor patio space below. A full-height wall of glass overlooking the Catskill Mountains offers spectacular views.

FACING PAGE BOTTOM: The stunning site of the home in upstate New York captures the dramatic surroundings of both the Hudson Valley and the Catskill Mountains.
Photographs by Jason Keen

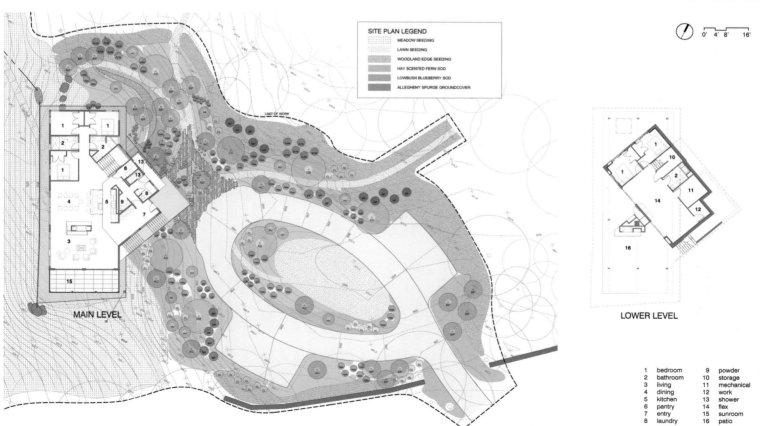

SITE PLAN LEGEND

MEADOW SEEDING
LAWN SEEDING
WOODLAND EDGE SEEDING
HAY SCENTED FERN SOD
LOWBUSH BLUEBERRY SOD
ALLEGHENY SPURGE GROUNDCOVER

0' 4' 8' 16'

LIMIT OF WORK

MAIN LEVEL

LOWER LEVEL

1	bedroom	9	powder
2	bathroom	10	storage
3	living	11	mechanical
4	dining	12	work
5	kitchen	13	shower
6	pantry	14	flex
7	entry	15	sunroom
8	laundry	16	patio

BELOW: This image shows the lakeside of the home and because of the precise shapes, has a Mondrian feel. Lighting and ceiling treatments were key when we designed this house—both catch your eye from the rear perspective. The house is in Wilnette, Illinois.

FACING PAGE: Quietly dramatic, the staircase in the entryway is the first thing you see when you step into the home. Its sculptural appeal deserves full attention and thus, there is no artwork or competing elements to draw away from it. The elegant, modern light fixture extends through three floors.
Photographs by Werner Straube Photography

Morgante-Wilson Architects

The principals at Morgante-Wilson approach architecture like you would a language. To understand it, you must learn the rules, and once you're fluent, the creativity begins. Started more than 30 years ago, the Illinois-based firm has become versed in a wide range of styles and is undoubtedly fluent. The team moves easily between design, construction, and renovation—but it doesn't stop there. Morgante-Wilson also includes an interior design group that creates custom furniture to suit the most specific needs.

Led by husband and wife Fred Wilson and Elissa Morgante, the firm designs homes that have one thing in common: livability. The houses are practical, comforting, and meant to be lived in. Each home speaks to the homeowners' specific needs and addresses their lifestyle. The entire process is an exchange of ideas, but begins by the principals listening to and understanding the homeowners.

BELOW TOP: We created the dining space to accommodate a wide range of guests—up to 30 to be exact. The table can expand 10 feet in both directions, making kids tables and extra seating obsolete on holidays. Intimate sitting areas appear on either side of the table, so conversation spaces are always an option.

BELOW BOTTOM: The fireplace takes center stage here, with an eye-catching push and pull of brick work. It's nestled in the screened-in porch on the north side of the home, which has heated floors. We lifted the fireplace so its geometrical patterns can be seen—and appreciated—from any seat in the room.
Photographs by Werner Straube Photography

BELOW TOP: The island is made from a walnut tree that was on the home's site. We wanted to incorporate it into the design, and after the tree dried, we saw how beautiful the heartwood was. Since the kitchen is the heart of the home, it seemed like the most fitting way to repurpose the tree.

BELOW BOTTOM: A lake view appears in every room on the back of the house, including the master bathroom. Motorized drapery gives the homeowners full privacy when necessary. Behind the tub, a dry-set marble wall has a noticeable vein that adds a diagonal element to the space.
Photographs by Werner Straube Photography

"It's imperative to understand the rules of architecture, so you know when to break them."
—Elissa Morgante

BELOW: When we built this house in Beaver Creek, Colorado, we were up against some strict building codes and architectural restrictions. Because of the mandated height limit, we carved a floor into the landscape to create the space that the homeowners wanted.

FACING PAGE TOP: Inside, skiers can relax and unwind after a day on the slopes. Floor-to-ceiling windows capture the full beauty of the surrounding mountains and have a ventilation feature on the bottom to let in fresh air.

FACING PAGE BOTTOM: With no neighbors, this home didn't have privacy concerns and the windows didn't need treatments. This lets plenty of sunshine in. Above the vanity, a window lets the natural light come through to the hidden toilet and shower, just behind it.
Photographs by Gibeon Photography

"Our style is rooted in history but leans toward contemporary. We're open to everything."
—Fred Wilson

FACING PAGE TOP: The homeowners of this Evanston, Illinois, house were enamored with a very specific high-end Italian cabinetry. Because of that, we prioritized the cabinetry in the budget and made practical, more cost-effective decisions in other areas of the kitchen. The standard, stainless-steel hood and puck lighting for example, make ideal complements to the cabinets without overspending.
Photograph by Jim Tschetter Photography

FACING PAGE BOTTOM: This was a full remodel, so we had to change the language of the home to something more modern that fit the personalities of the owners. The staircase has a linear, Alvar Aalto-like quality that can also be found on the home's street-facing façade. Elements of Scandinavian design that can be seen on the front of the home include clean lines and sleek, simplistic shapes.
Photograph by Jim Tschetter Photography

ABOVE & RIGHT: When homeowners in Winnetka, Illinois, wanted to change the vibe of their Tudor into something completely different, we obliged. Light played a key role to changing the space, and we snuck it in by adding windows just behind the cabinets. You can see the silhouette of the dishes as the light shines through. Modern elements such as this gave the kitchen a whole new feel. The large, grey steel beam was added to the façade and carried throughout the interior to support bearing walls that were removed, and a cast concrete countertop provides a strong edge to define the kitchen workspace.
Photograph by Werner Straube Photography

Snow Kreilich Architects

Though Snow Kreilich Architects doesn't design buildings to win awards, it has certainly won its share in the past 20-plus years. Founded in 1995, the Minneapolis-based practice was honored with the national 2018 AIA Architecture Firm Award, the highest honor bestowed on an architecture firm. One way the studio ensures design excellence is by committing that each project will be led by one or both of its design principals, Julie Snow and Matt Kreilich. There is also a rigorous focus on producing architecture that innovates and supports the client's aspirations and missions, as well as utilizing sustainable methods and preserving historic buildings whenever possible.

The design process at Snow Kreilich begins with thorough research to support its clients' pragmatic and intangible aspirations, leading to architecture that represents a precise ethos and mission. The work is grounded in the specifics of each site's context, intensifying the connection to place, history, culture, and nature. Through creative collaboration with engineering and construction teams, the studio also provides integrated building systems that are more effective, efficient, and durable. The studio's work has been published internationally, and Princeton Architectural Press has published the work in a series of monographs on emerging designers from around the world.

BELOW: The house is conceived as a sequential experience. The approach road curves through dense woods. A parking court is defined by the remnants of the former cottage, a barn, and playhouse. The portal framing views of the water punctuates the arrival at the residence.

FACING PAGE: Two overlapping forms, one clad in black stained cedar the other natural, form a broad portal that frames the lake view and creates an outdoor pool courtyard. The black volume which contains the main living area and master suite runs perpendicular to the lake. The long leg of the L sits on the ground with the short leg, the master suite, on top. The children's wing, defined in clear stained cedar siding, runs parallel to the shoreline, spanning from a small pool room across the portal and resting on the main living wing. The intersection of these two volumes is defined by vertical space, lit from a large skylight opening above. A black steel stair connects the three levels of the home.
Photographs Paul Crosby Architectural Photography

"Using restraint and minimal means, we pursue the inspired moments that architecture can bring to everyday use."
—Julie Snow

BELOW & FACING PAGE: Bells Woods sits on a 23-acre-site near Nashville, Tennessee, in an area rich with Southern tradition. We were inspired by the surrounding 19th-century stone walls—dry-stacked and crenellated with jagged lines—Antebellum plantation homes, and once-thriving farm structures. The modern home's hilltop perch rests behind a well-aged tobacco barn and the meandering drive circles through a pasture and up to the house through a densely forested grove.
Photographs by Farshid Assassi

Steven Ginn Architects

Steven Ginn Architects is a small firm with big design ideas. Founding principal Steven Ginn subscribes to a rigorous approach to excellence and believes that all successful projects should end with a happy homeowner. Steven and his close-knit team work collaboratively through the entire process to achieve a higher design standard. With a committed, client-focused approach, Steven's team is able to deliver unique and innovative buildings on time and on budget. They start every project by listening to the homeowner and thoroughly studying the site to take advantage of every opportunity.

Steven began Steven Ginn Architects in his native Omaha, Nebraska, but he developed his craft through extensive international travel and study. After completing his education at the University of Kansas and St. Louis' Washington University, Steven traveled to Africa, Asia, and Europe to learn about indigenous architecture and building techniques. While in Italy, he worked primarily on the design and restoration of castle estate homes. When he returned to the United States, he continued to develop his skillset by joining a number of well-known, award-winning firms and collaborating on a variety of project types. Today, Steven and his firm focus on residential projects, interior design, furniture design and religious, cultural and commercial designs. The firm's work can be found throughout Nebraska and the Midwest, including Iowa, South Dakota, and Tennessee.

ABOVE & LEFT: The expanses of glass make it obvious that this isn't a typical Southern mansion, yet somehow the house fits into this place and time. The exposed-timber structure, supporting the protective mass of shed roof, articulates its purpose with steel, emphasizing key elements. Rich wood tones contrast with jagged stone to create a contemporary and rustic feel. It's warm and inviting, appealing to the basic innate desire for shelter while revealing the heightened art of living.

FACING PAGE: We organized the house around two stone walls, loosely forming a skewed cross. The first wall runs parallel to a central old road, while the second runs perpendicular to the slope of the hill, dividing the house into quarters. Each quarter segments the house into different levels of privacy: entry, entertainment and living, master, and service. As you move through the spaces, you will notice they are organized around the demising walls, revealing themselves in layers.

Photographs by Farshid Assassi

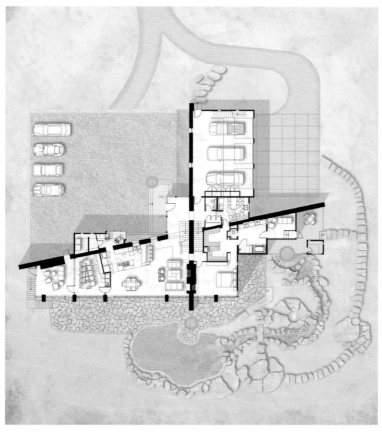

ABOVE & LEFT: The Woolworth kitchen renovation began with a long, narrow space that was cluttered with outdated décor, and it became a clean, contemporary space. The focal point of the kitchen is at the center island and provides wheelchair access for the homeowners' son. This island is fabricated of concrete and accented with black quartz and framed above with carved ceiling panels inspired by boiling water. The dynamic, boat-shaped island retains the wood texture from its casting and curves through the narrow space, allowing ease of use for wheelchair users.

FACING PAGE: For Hill House, the main objective was to preserve the look and feel of the projecting saddle ridge. The owners fell in love with the land exactly as it is and we didn't want to compromise that, so rather than building directly on the ridge, the house straddles it. Divided into two wings, the house is connected by a sun-soaked link. At the east, the public-facing wing greets visitors with an old bronze bell delicately suspended from a pair of cantilevered steel channels. The western wing withdraws from public view and projects into the thick canopy of trees.

Photographs by Farshid Assassi

"We strive to rethink the typical."
—Steven Ginn

BELOW: Nestled into the side of a mountain, Four Mile Canyon is a 3,063 square-foot, single-family home with a unique blend of styles. Inspired by the forms of mining structures, the house has an industrial ambiance both inside and out. We developed its overall character by adding contemporary elements to refine the look and feel. The resulting blend creates a house that is full of subtle details; rustic but not crude, high quality but not extravagant. It genuinely reflects the individuality of the owners whose vision drove the design.

FACING PAGE: The central form of the house is a linear vaulted space with an open living room and kitchen, where scissor trusses accentuate the dominant timber-frame structure that we articulated on both the exterior and the interior of the house.
Photographs by James Ray Spahn

Tabberson Architects

The fleeting moments of the sun's intersection on the horizon offer profound inspiration to Bill Tabberson, founder of Tabberson Architects. That's because, like the sun, the connection of a piece of architecture to its site is both universal and timeless. "The threshold of earth and sky gives form to all kinds of creativity," Tabberson says. And, his firm's mission is to create and build spaces that honor our place on the earth.

Such poetic inspiration has earned Tabberson Architects a national reputation for being at the forefront of the industry in addition to being specialists in timberframe design—a way of building that resonates with the natural beauty of the environment. Ultimately, Tabberson and his team know that timeless architecture is never arbitrary. It is created with passion, sweat, and tears; it speaks with clarity and it is intrinsically understood.

Because the wonder of dawn and dusk is so integral to Tabberson Architects' designs, architect Chris Simmons captures these themes and provides conceptual images to clients. With this, the firm is truly able to begin to communicate the magic of the moments that influence the architecture they create. And, it's one of the ways they continue to garner growing interest in their firm—even after more than 25 years in the industry.

"The fireball of the sun as it breaks through the horizon is magical; it illuminates our architectural visions that occupy the edge of the earth."
—Bill Tabberson

ABOVE: Located within eyesight of Yellowstone National Park, the Wapiti Tranquility home capitalizes on the natural beauty of the environment. The 4,384-square-foot dwelling is one of a kind, customized distinctly to both its surroundings and to the clients' lifestyle.

RIGHT: Through strategic site orientation, building massing, and spatial planning, we united the grandeur of the exterior environment with the interior.

FACING PAGE TOP: We designed M&M Ranch into the physical site— and the home's relationship to the earth is the main inspiration for its architectural form. We extensively studied the horizon and the effects of how the sun rises and sets, so that we could ensure its shared axis to the orientation of the building.

FACING PAGE BOTTOM: As this was already a magnificent site, our goal for the architecture of this 2,770-square-foot home was for it to blend seamlessly within the landscape.
Photographs by Chris Simmons

Borrero Architecture, page 301

Woody Friese Architect, page 373

Studio K Architects, page 359

SOUTHEASTERN US

BELOW: In keeping with the surrounding historic mill cottage residences, we moderated the scale of this 3,244-square-foot house by locating much of the structure below street level. As the home is situated on a sloping site, it was also designed to provide maximum daylight into the walk-out basement. The front balcony is a modern reinterpretation of the traditional, southern front porch.

FACING PAGE: The house's unique, primary cladding is comprised of a metal T-panel coated by Precoat Metals in PPG's Duranar® VARI-Cool™ paint system. This color-changing polychromatic paint is UV-responsive and shifts from a copper color to bright pinkish-orange depending upon the time of day and angle of the sun. It is an amazingly dynamic façade treatment.
Photographs by Fredrik Brauer Photography

Architectural Collaborative

Architectural Collaborative (Arcollab) is led by founding partners Lori Bork Newcomer, Joseph Smith, and Gabriel Comstock who are intimately involved in all aspects of the design for the projects they lead. However, at its core, the office is a collaborative studio environment where creative dialogue is encouraged and embraced in the search for the best design solutions. And this same approach is brought to the firm's relationships; they pride themselves on their communication skills with both the client and the contractor.

Arcollab strives to create inspired spaces and structures that are strongly rooted in a sense of place and grow from the natural and built environment that's around them, in effect responding to and being respectful of each project site. The team is fluent in styles ranging from the historic and neo-traditional to cutting-edge, modern design, but they ultimately believe that a return to thoughtful, regional design is one of the best ways to address the proliferation of ubiquitous architecture as well as environmental concerns.

With a creative process that includes research and experimentation, sustainability considerations, ongoing client collaboration, and the thoughtful articulation of details, they consistently create inspired spaces that positively impact the lives of the people moving within them.

TOP LEFT: The front of the home features stepped retaining walls that reveal a sunken garden and above-ground basement walls. An entry bridge allows access to the front door above the garden.

BOTTOM LEFT: The home possesses myriad outdoor living spaces, where the balconies and patios fully integrate outdoor and indoor living, with multi-level planters adding color and acting as privacy devices.

BELOW TOP: We designed a shed roof to provide passive solar daylighting into the main living spaces while also providing south-facing roofline for a PV array.

BELOW BOTTOM: The south side balcony features a Vari-Cool metal-clad bamboo planter which acts as both a privacy screen and shading device.

FACING PAGE TOP: Steeped in natural light, the minimalist kitchen reflects the aesthetic of the home's architecture by prioritizing sleek stainless steel, wood, and granite finishes. Dual islands were designed to provide separate preparation space for the vegetarian in the household.
Photographs by Fredrik Brauer Photography

FACING PAGE BOTTOM: The main living area is a modern, open-concept room with bright, white walls to reflect the natural light along with a two-sided, slate and heart-pine fireplace—and notably no TV. The space directly links to the outdoors through the sliding doors that lead onto the private patio.
Photograph by Architectural Collaborative

"Ultimately, the thoughtful articulation of light, form, and materials creates inspired spaces that maintain a sense of place."
—Lori Bork Newcomer

BELOW: Our goal was to design this house in a way that addresses its unique location while working in a language that's within the tradition of South Florida modern architecture. The front is designed to emphasize the entrance by positioning the openings and simple, smooth textures in such a way that focuses the attention on the transparent center of the house. The material palette is kept at a minimum and a series of layered planes allows us to both direct views and reduce the prominence of the garage doors. These doors are treated as another abstract surface that blends in with the adjacent walls, matching the color and texture.

FACING PAGE: The interior view of the master hallway, like many of the spaces inside, was designed to always end with a framed vista to provide visual connections to the outside and bring in natural light.
Photographs by Emilio Collavino

Borrero Architecture

For Alejandro Borrero of Borrero Architecture, there is no such thing as a small or big project—they are all viable opportunities to contribute to the improvement of the built environment. It is within that vision that the firm considers their work as part of a larger context, where spaces and buildings are all important to a community's quality of life. This vision dictates that the work is always approached responsibly and with an eye towards opportunities; it should be a design that accompanies life and can bring a sense of pleasure.

At Borrero Architecture, the goal is to always provide clients with personalized service and to work as a partner throughout the design process. The team values communication and integrity as much as creativity, design, and attention to detail. That's because they understand that what they do is not just an art and a science, it is above all a service—to the client, to the community, and hopefully to society at large.

The firm strives for excellence in all aspects of design. They take pride in their attention to detail and the ability to develop plans that are complete, comprehensive, and easy to navigate during construction. With local and international experience in a variety of building types and scales, their work extends beyond single-family residences with a portfolio that includes mixed-use, multi-family residential, and townhome developments as well as religious buildings, private universities, and corporate and industrial projects.

BELOW TOP: The rear of the house is all about "looking out"—and that includes this exterior covered porch that reflects the simple and open layout of the interior. The decision to site the house at an angle allowed for a larger backyard and pool.

BELOW BOTTOM: We incorporated the white frame feature as a nod to classic mid-century modern Florida architecture. While the front of the house is all about vertical elements that direct the view, the rear is horizontal to frame it. The house was placed at an angle in relation to the seawall in order to shield from some neighbors and provide longer views down the canal.
Photographs by Emilio Collavino

"We consider our work as part of a larger context, informed by local culture and materials—with the client always at the center of it all."
—Alejandro Borrero

BELOW TOP: We designed this expansive, modern one-story home around a tropical courtyard and pool. Signature Florida elements, such as deep overhangs and metal roofs, contrast the clean white of the exterior.

BELOW BOTTOM: All spaces revolve around the outdoors, with the open living area flowing into the lanai. We took particular care to ensure that the ceilings added light and movement to the space.
Photographs by Randy Tanner, Living Proof Real Estate Photography

BELOW TOP: Our goal was to emphasize the urban character of the neighborhood by presenting this open and compatible design along the street. We split the house into areas of one story and two stories, avoiding an overwhelming presence and breaking the roofline and scale. The composition of the exterior elevation was developed around the beautiful Ficus tree in the front. The windows on the bedrooms and stairway were placed to allow for different perspectives of the tree.

BELOW BOTTOM: The living, dining, and kitchen area is surrounded by operable doors and windows with the goal of providing a seamless transition between interior and exterior. In order to provide a variety of exterior experiences while protecting the interior glazed area from the effects of heat, we used different layers of shading features, such as deep porches, an aluminum pergola, and concrete overhangs. We designed these elements to provide a distinct appearance in the tradition of South Florida modern architecture.

Photographs by Randy Tanner, Living Proof Real Estate Photography

BELOW TOP: This interior view of the living, dining, and kitchen space, looking out towards the garden, also shows how we blurred the lines between the inside and the outside. We used a warm palette of rich woods to contrast with the cooler white and gray stone of the exterior; the juxtaposition emphasizes the transition between the domestic and the urban.
Photograph by Randy Tanner, Living Proof Real Estate Photography

BELOW BOTTOM: The top rendering is the street-facing west elevation of the house. The bottom rendering is the garden-facing east elevation.

"We don't see architecture only as the delivery of a finished product, but also as the meandering path to get us there. For us, the process is just as critical as the result."
—Alejandro Borrero

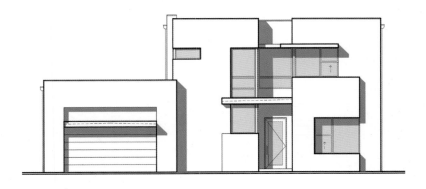

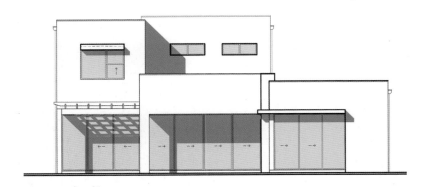

BELOW: We designed every aspect of this home, including the architecture, interiors, furnishings, and landscape design. The statement-making front façade is unique in its bold simplicity—from the front entry gate's functional sculpture, designed by artist Zach Oxman, to the angle of the front entry steps and roof line which are both complemented by materials of wood, metal, glass, and stucco. The entire house is an artistic statement.

FACING PAGE: Excitement was added to the courtyard with a simple geometric pattern of inlaid marble. The lush tropical landscaping creates a sense of place and privacy.
Builder: Gil Development, Miami, FL
Photographs by Kris Tamburello

Brown Davis Architecture & Interiors

Their shared passion for classic architecture, discerning environments, and extraordinary craftsmanship led Todd Davis and Rob Brown to create Brown Davis Architecture & Interiors in 1994. Since that time, their firm has designed an array of exceptional projects involving both modern and classical design as well as historic renovations. Their portfolio even includes two residences for President and Secretary of State Clinton and The British Embassy residence.

Offering comprehensive architectural, furniture design, interior and landscape design, Brown Davis envisions all elements in unison, with creative and bespoke architecture serving as the foundation of each project—from modern to transitional and traditional styles. Although their projects have no geographic boundaries, Miami's saturated hues, tropical landscapes, and design vibes influence the firm's bold aesthetic that resists conformity. For them, this uniquely American perspective fuses the traditional roots of classicism with an international, modern, and sensual vitality.

Brown, a gifted designer and colorist, creates custom palettes that harmonize and balance transitions among eclectic furnishings—always keeping comfort as an indispensable priority and an utmost luxury. Working closely with master artisans, Brown Davis designs bespoke furnishings, perfectly scaled for size and function. Interestingly enough, both Brown and Davis have MBAs, which contributes to their refined project management and fiscal responsibility. Coupled with design intelligence, the firm earns from their clients what they deem their most cherished honor: trust.

BELOW TOP: The architecture and the interiors of this home are meant to seamlessly integrate with the tropical exterior, with even the striking book-matched quartzite wall resonating with the foliage outside. The large walls of sliding glass doors likewise combine the indoors with the outdoors.

BOTTOM LEFT AND BOTTOM RIGHT: We wanted to continue the artistic theme beyond the front entry gate with this equally sculptural stainless steel and wood spiral staircase in the foyer that immediately and dramatically welcomes you to the home.
Builder: Gil Development, Miami, FL
Photographs by Kris Tamburello

BELOW TOP: We custom-designed the plaster ceilings specifically for this residence, where no detail was left untouched—from the under-step lighting in the foyer, to the custom dining table from the Brown Davis Exclusively for Keith Fritz furniture line, and the custom angled rugs. Over the dining table hang four vintage Murano glass chandeliers.

BELOW BOTTOM: In the master bedroom, vintage bedside tables and custom hand-painted silk wallpaper seamlessly resonate with the custom headboard, a Brown Davis design.
Builder: Gil Development, Miami, FL
Photographs by Kris Tamburello

"Elements like texture, light, and pattern can be artfully orchestrated for enduring impact, warmth, and harmony."
—Rob Brown

BELOW: Living at the Colleton River near Hilton Head, SC, incorporating the views of the golf course and water is paramount. Our design approach was to have all spaces lead to one other through the use of a glass sliding wall and use of the same, repeating materials and attention to detailing.

FACING PAGE: The use of Dominican Republic stone on the interior and exterior walls and floors provides the pallete and surface for the tranquil, Zen-like feeling that the owners desired in their magnificent home.
Photographs by Pam Singleton

Camens Architectural Group

When building homes in a beautiful setting, homeowners and many architects focus on the outdoors and bringing them in. Marc Camens, principal and founder of Camens Architectural Group, chooses to build homes in the opposite way, and the results are absolutely spectacular. Marc builds homes from the inside out by first learning about how his clients live, rather than developing a laundry list of rooms and features. He learns how they eat, entertain, cook, relax, and work at home. Then he considers the site and adapts the floorplan—based on the owners' lifestyles—to the site to integrate the two. Finally, he builds the exterior around the plan to envelop it. According to Marc, when an architect builds in the opposite way—taking the exterior into consideration first—they risk stuffing the interiors with rooms that the owners do not need.

It is with this approach in mind that Marc leads his team of architects to build distinctive residences that immediately feel like home. Homeowners are guided through every step of the design and building process and love watching their visions come to life. Fine details, from intricate millwork and decorative columns that transition between spaces, to leaded glass accents, and even accent lighting in kitchen cabinetry, are taken into account by the architects of Camens Architectural Group. The homes that result are breathtaking, well-built, and memorable, holding true to the firm's unofficial slogan: Listen to your dreams and we'll listen to you.

BELOW: The clean line mahogany stairwell and massive columns display quiet strength in the structure of this home.

FACING PAGE TOP: The beautiful view of the Pete Dye golf course with the Colleton Rivers is touched and captured through the sliding glass wall. This view is enhanced by the massive exposed open structure. This can only be achieved by designing the home from the inside out.

FACING PAGE BOTTOM: Clean lines of the open kitchen flow right off of the living area and onto the porch.
Photographs by George Guttenburg

"Sensitive transitions from one room to another create emotional transitions that people crave."
—Marc Camens

BELOW & FACING PAGE: The Japanese concept of shakkei, or borrowed scenery, informs the design of this Virginia Beach house, which was completed in 2016. The site is characterized by a strong sense of horizontality, formed by the foreground waterway of Linkhorn Bay, the line of woods on the opposite shore, and the sky. A linear fountain strikes a line along the entry path and appears to slide beneath the house, reappearing as an exterior pool at the far side of the foyer. A trellis complements the fountain and pool by extending the view through the house, while concrete walls reinforce the property's lines. In tandem with the green agenda of Hays + Ewing, the gardens designed by Kennon Williams Landscape Studio utilize native species to reduce the need for irrigation. *Photographs by Prakash Patel*

Hays + Ewing Design Studio

A team since 2004, with more than 30 years of collective experience between them, Christopher Hays and Allison Ewing are leaders in the green design movement. Integrating techniques such as cooling through natural ventilation, rainwater collection, and harnessing energy from the sun, the duo have become experts at harmonizing buildings with their surrounding environment. They believe that enduring architecture springs from a deep understanding of the place, the needs of the project, and the desires of the client, all the while directed by ecological principles and utilizing sustainable best practices.

A wide variety of projects, in both type and scale, have allowed them to tackle diverse projects and places with a clear vision that's specific to each. With a global architectural background, both Allison and Christopher have lived and worked in Europe and Asia in addition to the U.S., and both have participated in award-winning projects with such bold-face names as Cesar Pelli, Renzo Piano, and William McDonough. Their firm primarily serves Virginia and North Carolina, but has undertaken projects across the U.S., in Canada, and Europe.

BELOW: LED lighting throughout means the energy loads from lighting are minimal. Sustainably harvested Forest Stewardship Council-certified wood was used for framing lumber and all cabinetry and finish wood.

FACING PAGE TOP: The 16-foot-tall great room, with its floor-to-ceiling glass walls, appears to float above the pool and offers views of the bay on three sides. Utilizing triple-pane windows, the house is finely tuned to be extremely energy efficient. With concrete and stone floors, the heat from the winter is stored and released throughout the day. Geothermal wells provide clean and renewable energy to the home.

FACING PAGE CENTER: A series of terraces further engage the views: A ground-floor terrace wraps the living room while a second-floor covered porch provides a birds-eye perspective. Da Motta Design interiors complement the site's breathtaking beauty with furnishings that draw from nature's colors and textures.

FACING PAGE BOTTOM: Privacy glass in the master bath switches from clear to opaque by applying voltage. Marble is introduced in select rooms to complement the minimalist palette of concrete, limestone and dark finishes.
Photographs by Prakash Patel

317

BELOW TOP: This Zen, net-zero house in Faber, Virginia, celebrates the importance of the "rituals" of everyday life for the owner and her many visitors. The architect set out to design a self-sufficient green home that integrates the rhythm of the owner's daily schedule with the spirit of the land and its micro-climate.

BELOW BOTTOM: The roof form is the primary defining element; in one calligraphic gesture, it rises from the south up to a third-floor gallery, cascading down on the north to create a porte cochere.
Photographs by Prakash Patel

BELOW TOP: THE house is sited on a hilltop to take advantage of the surrounding views, particularly to the west toward the Blue Ridge Mountains, as well as the prevailing breezes that sweep across the hillside. A modern interpretation of the traditional "widow's walk," the third-floor observatory has windows on all sides. The observatory acts as a solar chimney, helping to regulate the temperature of the home through ventilation.

BELOW BOTTOM: The roof shape creates a continuous flow for the interior spaces, from the ground level up to the observatory, and facilitates a natural air flow. The living, dining, and kitchen area is suffused with daylight from the east, south, and west.
Photographs by Prakash Patel

"Beauty is not a trade-off for green design—beauty is essential to a building's long-term survival and therefore its environmental impact."
—Allison Ewing

BELOW: We developed the Ballantrae Court residence as a seasonal home in a South Florida golf community, responding to both the client's desire for a modern design while embracing the context of Florida living and the community's aesthetic requirements. The metal roof cladding along with natural stone walls and wood ceilings and decks reflect the vernacular building traditions of the area. Extensive window walls afford seamless integration and visual connection to the outdoors, with the back of the house defined by pavilions that extend into the landscape and look out to the golf course beyond.

FACING PAGE: At the main entry, the louvers, water garden, and river rocks create a sense of tranquility.
Photographs by Robin Hill

KZ Architecture

Jaya Kader, founding principal of KZ Architecture, has always been passionate about beauty and how it is expressed in nature, but it wasn't until she took an architectural history class in college that she knew how to manifest her core interests of art, humanities, nature, and culture—and the rest is, well, history. She has worked on numerous projects including public libraries, schools, municipal centers, houses of worship, residences, and resorts. As a Costa Rica native, her travels have afforded the opportunity to experience world-class architecture and understand the higher calling of her craft.

Many have described KZ Architecture projects as tropical modern, but rather than being confined to a particular style, she simply believes her work to be humanistic and in tune with nature, mindfulness, and spirituality. Her best advice is always to start with a blank slate and let go of any preconceived notions of what a building should be. Jaya has also been an advocate for sustainable design since the inception of her firm in 2003—one of her projects was the first LEED certified residence in Miami. Her firm exemplifies how to use the power of design to extend sustainability across environmental, social, and economic concerns.

Above everything, though, Jaya considers the most important technique of her work to be good listening. Understanding her clients' needs is the key to creating projects that merit the purpose they are meant to serve—and, indeed, the process of helping others manifest their dreams through creativity and design is what she enjoys most.

321

BELOW: Spacious, distinct exterior living spaces in the rear courtyard, including terraces, porches, and balconies, continuously connect the inside to the outside and extend the interaction between the landscape and the architecture.

FACING PAGE TOP: These louvers in the front of the home provide privacy from the street and modulate the southeastern morning sunlight.

FACING PAGE CENTER: A large central space integrates the living, den, kitchen, and dining area, all with extension to the outdoor covered spaces. Materials and finishes weave in and out of the house, with metal and stone clad walls as well as tongue and groove ceilings that consistently define the interior and exterior spaces.

FACING PAGE BOTTOM: The main entry to the house invites natural sunlight into the space, creating a play of light and shadow, with the sculptural wood and stainless steel staircase.
Photographs by Robin Hill

BELOW & FACING PAGE: Located in a mountain resort community that skirts the southernmost edge of the Blue Ridge Mountains, this single-family home has both a nested and a perched quality—a result of the structure's differing relationships to stratified stone retaining walls. From the street side, the house appears to cling to the terroir of the site. On the view side, the primary volume of the structure cantilevers out over the long stone wall. The design integrates locally sourced materials wherever possible; cedar is the primary cladding material selected for its durability, workability, and abundance in the Southeast. The retaining walls are sheathed in Swannanoa stone from the closest quarry in western North Carolina. The roof is a simple standing-seam low-luster galvanized metal, used in the region for generations due to its low cost and durability. All landscape plant materials are native to the region, eliminating the need for an irrigation system.
Photographs courtesy of LS3P

LS3P Associates Ltd

Architecture, interiors, and planning firm LS3P has been designing extraordinary, award-winning custom homes for more than five decades. LS3P's residential design team believes that everyone deserves to live in a well-designed home. A home should reflect the client's unique identity; the architects are people first, and designers second—a mindset that underscores just how much small details matter.

The goal at LS3P is to get to know clients through an established process of active listening, and then carefully craft the design to fit the vision revealed by that listening process. The residential design team, led by architect John Edwards, takes pride in exceeding clients' expectations in providing thoughtful, timeless, and creative home designs.

LS3P credits its success to the longstanding relationships its designers have built with clients on projects of all sizes, from tiny renovations to new custom homes. LS3P's portfolio is as diverse as its homeowners. With a rich portfolio of both traditional and modern homes, the architects see those traditional roots as a contributor in defining the broader southern regional modernism reflected in LS3P's work.

Recognizing that great design is the result of a way of thinking and is not restricted to a particular housing type, size, or style, LS3P's legacy of distinctively designed homes reflects the dreams and aspirations of clients from mid-century to next century. The team's work can be found throughout the coastal and mountain regions of the Carolinas and Georgia.

BELOW & FACING PAGE: The 3,000-square-foot house belongs to a noted maritime photographer. He wanted to create a home that, while inland, would be reminiscent of the simple boathouse buildings that formed the basis of his professional documentary photographic work. The result is an "architecture of artful resistance" in a planned community where strict design guidelines are geared toward the traditional, romantic architectural styles. Rather than being constrained by these guidelines, the project espouses modern regional romanticism that instead celebrates the rich formal and material traditions of vernacular buildings characterized by modesty, simplicity, and clarity.
Photographs courtesy of LS3P

BELOW & FACING PAGE: When LS3P took on a three-phase renovation to an existing 4,000-square-foot suburban residence, the work touched all aspects of the home, including the interior, exterior, landscaping, and technology. The original structure, an abandoned mid-century modern home, had fallen into serious disrepair. The intent during the renovation was to celebrate the home's modern roots while undressing and redressing the structure using current materials and methods that lent durability and enhanced character. *Photographs courtesy of LS3P*

"For us, creating the modern residence is a celebration of context. That includes revealing both the personal context—which is the essence of one's lifestyle—and sensibly incorporating cues provided by the place you're building."
—John Edwards, AIA

ABOVE & LEFT: When LS3P was asked to update a weary and worn 1980s country-style kitchen in this Charleston Single House, the owner embraced the idea that the modern art of cooking could be enhanced by a modern kitchen. The spartan lines of the contemporary kitchen meshed comfortably with the spartan lines of the Single House and are unified by the juxtaposition of white against deeply patinated hardwoods.
Photographs by Inspiro8.com

"*Where we practice in the Southeast, keeping ideas about modern home design innovative and fresh is more than just a form and function proposition. It requires a studious awareness of our region's earliest architectural heritage—a tradition of building simply and elegantly. Much of our work is about the expression of new homes in a way that honors these traditions.*"

—John Edwards, AIA

BELOW: Our goal was to create a gated enclave of 66 ultra-luxurious contemporary homes—the first modern luxury home development in South Florida.

FACING PAGE: Open floor plans with modern elevations highlight the architecture while outdoor living spaces, including roof top terraces, accentuate the tropical living environment.
Photographs by DEVTOV Group, LLC

Pascual Perez Kiliddjian & Associates

Since its founding in 1985, Pascual, Perez, Kiliddjian & Associates (PPK) has focused on its clients, offering planning and architectural services across the state of Florida and beyond, from the Bahamas to Central America. Three partners form the leadership at PPK—together, they bring more than 50 years of experience—and they lead a team of 23 architects and planners of diverse nationalities and levels of experience.

The design philosophy of PPK is based on solid principles of innovation, flexibility, and efficiency; values that have allowed them to prevail in such a competitive market. Their goal is to achieve a balance between efficiency and elegance in each of their projects, integrating the best aspects of current construction techniques along with cutting-edge design.

Clients seek out PPK because of the comprehensive services the firm provides. From the initial planning stage, PPK incorporates its market knowledge and experience in architectural design and efficient construction—a strategy that has been the foundation of ensuring the value and identity of each project the firm completes.

Presently, PPK is working throughout South Florida and the Caribbean, two areas that are considered to be some of the best regions for real estate development. Within this region, an international market is seeking sustainable modern designs, tropical outdoor living areas, and luxury amenities. So, the ultimate vision is a modern-contemporary style with climate-conscious detailing—not only for the outdoor living spaces and façades, but also in the development of floor plans with interior spaces that facilitate a better relationship with the exterior.

BELOW: When you think of entertaining or relaxation during the warm-weather months, homes at the beach or in the country immediately come to mind. But, the homes in this gated community can be enjoyed year-round and include all the amenities of an alfresco retreat, including ample green open spaces, in a secluded urban setting.

FACING PAGE TOP: The architectural language established for this development lets homeowners enjoy the benefits of contemporary living while allowing them to customize the finishes and materials that make their home their own.

FACING PAGE CENTER: The open floor plan is highly functional for entertaining as well as day-to-day living—and directly connects to the outdoors. Having both formal and casual living and dining spaces is an ideal arrangement that results in useful modern spaces.

FACING PAGE BOTTOM: This expansive roof terrace might as well be an outdoor home, with its dining space, cozy seating areas, and unforgettable views.
Photographs by DEVTOV Group, LLC

BELOW: With tall ceilings and an emphasis on natural light, we prioritized architectural design that integrates both the interior and exterior spaces; the ability to be connected to the outside while inside is very desirable—especially in the climate of South Florida.

FACING PAGE TOP: The element of customization and creating visual diversity among each home is essential to the identity of modern architecture—and to this development.

FACING PAGE BOTTOM: The project conforms with National Green Building Standards while providing practices for the design, construction, and certification of new energy-efficient single-family homes, connecting each resident to their home to help them live more intelligently by utilizing the newest technological advances in climate-conscious luxury.
Photographs by Andie Salinas

BELOW: A floating spa punctuates the pool in this large sun terrace, which doubles as a great entertaining space.

FACING PAGE: Crisp lines and simple forms shape a second-floor veranda with ocean views.
Photographs by Sargent Photography

Smith and Moore Architects

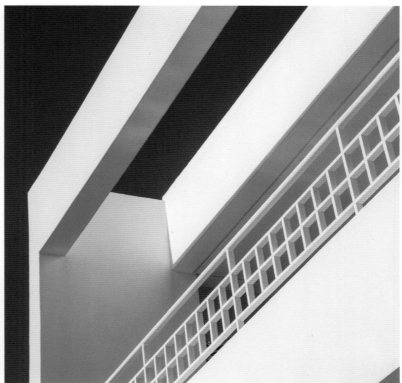

The four partners of the award-winning Smith and Moore Architects—Harold Smith, Jonathan Moore, Peter Papadopoulos, and Daniel Kahan—have built their reputation on combining contemporary construction techniques with tested architectural traditions. The result? Solutions that are not only timeless but meet the needs of modern-day living for their clients, which span residential and boutique commercial projects around the world.

The firm, founded in 1984, focuses primarily on the island of Palm Beach, always taking care to work the ocean views and plentiful sunlight into its designs. The architects approach each project in a holistic manner, understanding the variety of architectural traditions and contextual relationships that each new enterprise presents. Traditional methods of design, such as hand-drawing and model-making, join forces with cutting-edge technology, computer design tools, 3-D modeling, and 3-D printing. They also work closely with landscape and interior designers to create homes with a sense of place and permanence, combining beauty, comfort, quality, and functionality. Whether focusing on new construction or historic renovations and restorations, Smith and Moore is committed to designing projects that respect and enhance their surroundings.

BELOW TOP: Steel doors establish the rhythm and symmetry at a classical modern estate in Palm Beach.
Photograph by Sargent Photography

BELOW BOTTOM: Living spaces surround a courtyard and reflecting pool at a tropical modern oceanfront estate.
Rendering courtesy of Smith and Moore Architects

FACING PAGE TOP: Lush landscaping and a layered façade form a brutalist entry to an oceanfront estate, opening to crystalline sea views beyond.
Rendering courtesy of Smith and Moore Architects

FACING PAGE BOTTOM: A floating wood stair and sliding glass wall open to a large loggia and ocean views at a modern beach house.
Photograph by Michael Stavaridis

"Let the design work with the site, not dominate it."
—Jonathan Moore

BELOW & FACING PAGE: TipTop Haus is a nod to Sarasota's midcentury modern architecture that blended passive environmental elements with the dynamic components particular to the city's culture. The clean lines and minimalist approach to the home's design highlight the lush surroundings of the site.
Photographs by Ryan Gamma Photography

Solstice Planning and Architecture

Jonathan Parks, AIA, is very much connected to where he lives, and it has both inspired and defined him as an architect. Located in Sarasota, Solstice Planning and Architecture was the result of Jonathan's childhood visits to his aunt's Florida home in the 1970s, where he admired the distinct look and feel of the local regional architecture. The city has a specific architectural history that captured—and maintained—his attention.

Led by renowned architects Ralph Twitchell and Paul Rudolph in the 1950s, Sarasota experienced a surge in modern design throughout the midcentury. The structures showed off modern design features, using natural materials, sleek lines, and geometrical forms, and expressed an appreciation for functionality. You couldn't find anything quite like this in the U.S. at the time.

Jonathan began Solstice Planning and Architecture more than 15 years ago and has built the practice on his strong reputation—he and his team didn't advertise for years. Solstice is known for clarity of concept and quality of work. In fact, Jonathan has received more than 70 regional and national honors. His goal is to design memorable, timeless homes, with emphasis placed not only on the tangible, such as volume and shape, but also on immaterial elements of transparency, light, and space.

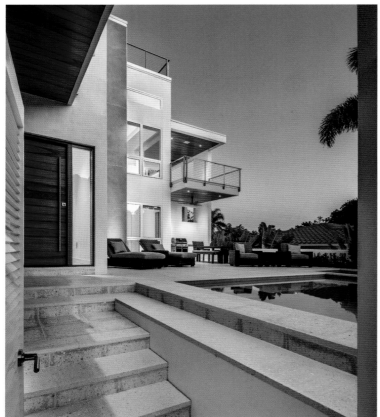

"I believe in an
'architecture of ideas.'
There is a thought behind
everything that we do."
—Jonathan Parks, AIA

"If properly done, design can change the way you live."
—Jonathan Parks, AIA

ABOVE, RIGHT, & FACING PAGE: The home features a refined entrance on the lower level, with a living space that helps to push the flow of traffic toward the pool deck. The stairs serve as the home's central point and extend through the height of the home. Using modern components and simple finishes, the home maintains its warmth because of the natural material selection and the constant sightlines to the exterior surroundings. An 800-square-foot rooftop space lets residents see the city's skyline, Sarasota Bay, and the Gulf of Mexico.
Photographs by The Greg Wilson Group

BELOW & FACING PAGE: The elevated pool for the Compass Haus interplays with the home and extends the visible exterior space beyond the setbacks. A roof terrace is accessed by an interior stair and provides a private outdoor area in close proximity to the water views. The landscape was critical to this project. Several of the larger species were in place and nursed to health during construction, while the rest of the landscape was intentionally set to lend scale and to soften the rigid forms of the architecture, all while ensuring that views were not obstructed, but enhanced. Only Florida-friendly, drought-tolerant plants were used and site permeability was maximized.
Photographs by Ryan Gamma Photography

BELOW: The home is closely bound by waterfront setback lines and is elevated one story to meet flood regulations. The design intent was to reconnect the house to the exterior and take advantage of the waterfront views.

FACING PAGE: The kitchen is the centerpiece of the home and the open plan is designed to connect kitchen to the entry, living, and dining areas. A distinctive modern stairway orchestrates the daily journey from public to private spaces with a playful curve and the use of solid-wood treads. The exposed concrete wall that supports the stairs and the roof will provide passive cooling through the use of thermal mass.
Photographs by Ryan Gamma Photography

"*Historically, architecture is a portrait of who we are. Society is defined by it.*"
—Jonathan Parks, AIA

"We strive to have our work provide a positive impact on the communities in which the project resides."
—Jonathan Parks, AIA

ABOVE, LEFT, & FACING PAGE: The Element House is located on a narrow lot that sits inside a flood zone on Sarasota Bay. The property had challenges to overcome, including constructing this project within 10 feet from the neighbor's home. In order to define sightlines away from the neighboring property and to take advantage of the open water views, we proposed an upside-down design, lifting living areas to the upper levels and locating guest rooms and children's rooms on the ground floor, alongside an informal family area. Above that foundation, the upper main living level includes the master bedroom, an open kitchen area adjacent to the main staircase, and the dining and living spaces. The higher you climb in this home, the better the views become, culminating with an upper-level social space with exterior deck. The project is one of the highest rated sustainable houses built in the country, with a HERS Index of -26, which is the third lowest score recorded in Florida.
Photographs by Ryan Gamma Photography

Studio9 Architecture

A room is seldom static space. And how a room artfully engages with other spaces through movement, light, order, and the outdoors is what inspires the team at Studio9 Architecture, including principals Jason Faulkner, AIA, and Craig Davisson, AIA.

The firm is a provider of planning, design, and delivery solutions for the built environment with architecture and interior design services as their core business. But, they also provide strategic partnerships with skilled professionals to add further resources and capabilities to their portfolio.

Studio9 believes that the best architecture is simple, clean, and expressive; it does not become dated with any particular style. For them, architecture should stand on fundamental principals.

Their ultimate goal is to interpret clients' needs in an artistic manner that far exceeds expectations. This is what is most rewarding to them—along with seeing their projects come to life as a contribution to the communities in which they work.

BELOW: The final phase included an entire waterside expansion with movable glass walls, outdoor kitchen, saltwater pool, terrace, hardscape and pool house.

FACING PAGE: An expansive deck (top) accommodates year-round outdoor living. The water views, glimpsed from the deck (center), are stunning at this property. A wine room (bottom) is an elegant custom feature of the home.
Photographs by Douglas J. Eng Photography

*"Our conviction that good design contributes
to better living is at our core."*
—Craig Davisson

ABOVE: The Faulkner Residence is located on a half-acre of land at the water's edge; the site fronts a country road that was once orange groves and is now residential. The design concept for this residence was based on three things: maximizing views, accommodating the resident's daily life, and using conventional building materials to meet a tight budget. The second phase allowed for a detached workshop to accommodate the space, machinery, and tools for vintage automotive restoration, woodworking, and metals.

LEFT: The house plan is unconventionally stacked with living and dining areas and the kitchen located on the second level and bedrooms on the first. The second floor, accessed by an exterior and interior stairway, has panoramic views of the adjacent tributary and surrounding woods. Locating the living areas on the second floor allows for a 14-foot interior volume and south-facing clerestory windows for maximum daylight exposure.

FACING PAGE TOP: Together with the homeowner, Studio9 explored expanded design solutions that went far beyond the conventional but still resonated in a sophisticated and contemporary manner—from the inside out.

FACING PAGE BOTTOM: The kitchen is small and functional with smart design elements including built-in storage and a refrigerator nook to maximize space. *Photographs by Douglas J. Eng Photography*

BELOW: This single-family house in Miami has a really open view out to the Biscayne Bay, so we wanted to maximize that view with a massive outdoor living area. We carefully designed the vanishing edge spa and pool to look like raised cubes of water, visually linking them with the water and bringing the bay closer to the house.

FACING PAGE: At the main entrance, we built a glass floor over a water feature to unite the front with the outdoor living area at the back of the house. The tall glass entry wall looks straight through to the back of the house and the view out to the bay.
Photographs by Michael Stavaridis

Studio K Architects

Krsto Stamatovski, AIA, opened Studio K in 2002 after working at architectural firms both internationally and within the U.S. Not long after, he won the AIA People's Choice Design Award—and his firm has been making waves ever since, designing a variety of projects, including single and multi-family custom residential, commercial, restaurant, and hospitality architecture as well as interiors.

But, the vast majority of their projects are high-end, custom single-family residences across the country, from Miami to Manhattan, Colorado to California, the Hamptons, Idaho, and beyond—many of which they design as second and third residences for repeat clients.

Indeed, the firm considers their client interaction and collaboration a key strength, together creating the best possible living environment for each person's specific needs and lifestyle. Likewise, they are continually striving to design innovative, aesthetically pleasing spaces that seamlessly weave into the local vernacular and environment.

The Studio K team is a family—literally and figuratively—with Krsto serving as head architect, and his two daughters, Valentina and Violeta, as architect and interior designer, respectively. They work together to produce statement-making properties that withstand the test of time and look beautiful many years down the road.

"We love to focus on breaking the barrier between what is inside and outside to maximum effect."
—Krsto Stamatovski

ABOVE: Natural light plays a big role inside the home; the back elevation is completely glass. The two-story window wall blurs the lines between the indoor living room and its extension outdoors.

RIGHT: Right from the entrance, the foyer offers a view straight out towards the water.

FACING PAGE TOP: The two cantilevered terraces with glass balconies create outer space for the second floor without obstructing the views. For a sleek, streamlined look, we paired black and gray stone mosaic and polished granite throughout the exterior.

FACING PAGE BOTTOM: The home might as well be a resort with its lounge-worthy outdoor living space. We were lucky that the back of the house is oriented to the east, so the sun isn't as harsh in the afternoon.
Photographs by Michael Stavaridis

"Rather than being trendy, the goal is to be classic, yet innovative; to design something that looks beautiful after many years down the road."
—Krsto Stamatovski

ABOVE: In this penthouse, we designed a complete build-out of the space, from the layout of the rooms to the interiors. This niche family area makes an impact with a floating TV between glass pillars. The stepped ceiling and recessed lights hide all the mechanical vents and speakers for a polished finish.

ABOVE RIGHT: Throughout the penthouse, we worked to maximize the nearly 360-degree-view of the intercoastal waterways, ocean, and city. In the kitchen, the two-sided bar does just that, with seating positioned to look outside.

RIGHT: In the formal dining room, one of the most eye-catching features is a wine room constructed of wave-shaped wood, echoing the water outside. Equally enticing is the mesh chandelier that is almost like fine jewelry, draped above the handmade dining table.

FACING PAGE TOP: We designed this glass-enclosed dining area with a 360-degree-view as a uniquely striking feature for the massive outdoor living space.

FACING PAGE BOTTOM: The office looks out onto the terrace and ocean, again taking advantage of the dynamic view.
Photographs by Carmel and Robert Brandley

BELOW: Located in the heart of the leafy and laid-back enclave of Coconut Grove, a neighborhood just south of downtown Miami, this residence was designed to serve as a sanctuary from the hustle and bustle of the nearby city. White and ash gray stucco contrasts with ipe wood on the front façade.

FACING PAGE: The expanse of tall glazing on both the north and south elevations pours natural light into the double-height living space inside.
Photographs by Miles Abalia

Trussoni Architecture Group

One of Dr. Matthew Trussoni's favorite quotes is from 20th century visionary and inventor Buckminster Fuller who said, "When I'm working on a problem, I never think about beauty. I think only how to solve the problem. But when I have finished, if the solution is not beautiful, I know it is wrong."

Indeed, his namesake firm, Trussoni Architecture Group, finds meaning in both creating beautiful spaces and finding solutions to make people's lives better in the process. As such, they work across a variety of disciplines, including architecture, interior design, engineering, and construction.

Dr. Trussoni's creativity combined with his background and experience as a licensed architect, engineer, and contractor is what really sets him — and his firm — apart. They can both design and build innovative architecture for their clients, where contemporary style comes together with the thoughtful integration of sustainability.

They are inspired by the freedom to create and the gratification of watching that creation come to life. But, ultimately, they want their work to evoke a feeling; for them, it's all about the emotional connection a person gains from a space. That is truly their mission — and something they succeed at, time and again.

BELOW: Both interior and exterior spaces collaborate to provide an easy flow between each other and create a breathable, inviting home that accommodates daily family living as well as sophisticated entertaining.

FACING PAGE TOP: The floating staircase enhances the light and airy flow of this tropical oasis. The floor plan purposefully draws the eye towards the lush native landscape at the back of the property, dotted with coconut palms as well as a shimmering pool.

FACING PAGE MIDDLE: Strong, clean, and sleek lines of the reinforced concrete roof slabs accentuate the pull towards the greenery outside and the walls of sliding doors provide ample access to the outdoor entertaining spaces surrounding the pool and covered dining area.

FACING PAGE BOTTOM: Envisioned as a serene and relaxed space, the master bedroom's full-height windows and sliding glass doors provide views of the lush canopy for which Coconut Grove is known.
Developed by Urban Link Developers
Photographs by Miles Abalia

BELOW: The lush tropical surroundings of Miami's Coconut Grove neighborhood played a central role in the design methodology of this newly constructed home as did the intense South Florida sunshine and balmy climate. The front façade is clad in native coral stone and punctuated by the sky-blue eyebrows over each window to alleviate the heat of the southern-facing exposure.

FACING PAGE TOP: An inviting front porch with its large planting area, garden wall, and wood ceilings creates a cool and comfortable outdoor room. Together, the wood, stone, and clean lines create a tropical modern residence.

FACING PAGE BOTTOM: In the main room, we brought Miami's outdoor appeal inside the house with north-facing doors and two-story windows that look out to the pool. The double-height space was designed to showcase a family heirloom: an antique Venetian chandelier..
Photographs by Miles Abalia

BELOW: South Florida's lifestyle emphasizes the harmony of cool interior spaces with lush and inviting outdoor elements. This home's unique plan connects all of the spaces to each other with an easy flow and warm contemporary balance that's just as perfect for entertaining as it is for a quiet family evening in the garden.

FACING PAGE TOP: The wood from the stair line provides a warm and soft contrast to modern white walls. The operable clerestory windows above open to provide natural stack ventilation. Passive design strategies and energy efficiency combined with the solar array on the roof make this a net-zero energy home.

FACING PAGE CENTER: Large sliding doors open to the pool and a coral stone deck, providing an extension of the interior space into the outdoor realm. A six-panel mural, painted by the homeowner's father-in-law, is displayed in the dining room.

FACING PAGE BOTTOM: Wood ceilings and accents bring a calm and cozy experience to the kitchen and family room. We juxtaposed the white lacquer cabinetry and marble countertops in the culinary space with a custom wood breakfast table and blue dining chairs
Developed by Trussoni Architecture Group
Photographs by Miles Abalia

BELOW & FACING PAGE: *MASSING* is a three-story modern residence located on the canals of Coral Ridge, Fort Lauderdale, that totals more than 7,500 square feet of indoor living space with five bedrooms, five bathrooms, two guest baths, a separate three-story cabana, plus an additional 1,200 square feet of covered outdoor living space. We started the design process by utilizing the simple principles of general size, shape, and form and created vertical massing walls as the framework for the glass box reading room. Cladding features include elements of coreten iron and steel porcelain panels, and natural ledgestone quartzite to offset the stark white stucco. A private elevator provides access to all three levels, including the home theater with private bar and cigar deck. The bar is treated with rosewood veneers with book matching Michelangelo marble slabs and floating-glass tops. Veneered wood beams and LED strip lights add the final touches to the third-floor experience.
Photographs by Rosky Images

Woody Friese Architecture

According to Woody Friese, architecture must be viewed as living art. Growing up, he idolized modern architects such as Richard Meier and Frank Gehry for their abstract approach, and knew he'd found his passion when he took his first drafting class at 13. He wanted, like these men before him, to create structures for generations of people to appreciate. In 1993, he completed school from the University of South Florida as the youngest student with a master's degree in architecture and opened his own award-winning firm, Friese Design Group, four years later.

But a catastrophic ATV accident in 2005 left Woody a quadriplegic. He closed his firm and spent the next six years undergoing intensive physical and occupational therapy, eventually regaining the use of his hands and—thanks to a close friend and colleague—returned to the work that he loves. He joined VDG Architecture as the principal architect and lead designer in 2011. Now working under his own firm again, Woody offers his clients complete architectural design and site planning utilizing the latest 3-D walk-through technology. With this, homeowners can see their future house and experience Woody's distinct, artistic modern design before it's even built.

With the theory that "A unique design for an innovative mind," Woody believes you cannot have impressive architecture without bold clients. He understands that a truly great residence not only projects a vibrant impression but works well for the people that live there. Watching his clients settle into their new living work of art is his greatest joy.

BELOW: The ground floor features a two-story great room for dining and wine tastings, with an open butane fireplace. The house also boasts a semi-detached, three-story cabana house which has a ground-floor kitchen, second-floor gym, and top-floor guest suite. LED lighting technology enhances all the interior and exterior spaces to provide an even, glowing effect.

FACING PAGE TOP: The most prominent design feature is the second-floor floating master bathroom. My team and I used large, cantilevered steel beams to allow this space to float above the roof garden on top of the garage.

FACING PAGE CENTER: The kitchen and interiors, created by Rocio Carbonell, include solid rovere termocotto wood cabinets with unique marquina quartz slabs. The ceiling was designed as three-dimensional with alternating slopes.

FACING PAGE BOTTOM: The master spa includes a rain-shower head, body sprays, and adjoining steam chamber. Finishes included Italian porcelain floors and ming green marble slabs.
Photographs by Rosky Images

BELOW & FACING PAGE: *ARTISTRY* is located in the Las Olas area of Fort Lauderdale. This infill site was only 67-and-a-half-feet-wide, on both the main street and the alley, and provided me and my team with a unique design opportunity. The owner's criteria of natural light and open spaces with a sense of privacy dictated a formal drive court in the front with garages off of the alley. Creating a central outdoor pool courtyard became the focal point for all of the interior spaces, achieved through floor-to-ceiling pocketing sliding glass doors. These gave the homeowners a high level of control and allow them to manipulate the space while enjoying the abundant sunlight. For additional privacy and entertaining, a rooftop terrace provided more than 1,000 square feet to gaze on the downtown skyline.
Photographs by Barkin-Gilman Group

BELOW & FACING PAGE TOP: Because the owner is an affluent art collector, he wanted me to capture the essence of entering a modern art gallery. Upon entering the residence, the free-form staircase creates the invitation up to the art gallery loft. This curvilinear staircase was poured of solid concrete and wrapped with marble flooring and a custom aluminum tube railing. Within the three stories and 7,200 square feet you'll find four bedrooms, five full bathrooms, an entertainment room with full bar, the second-floor art gallery loft, and a rooftop terrace with elevator access.

FACING PAGE CENTER: The art on display can be seen from all open spaces on the ground floor.

FACING PAGE BOTTOM: Symmetry was created in the master bathroom by allowing for private floating vanities to appear on either side of the centralized spa tub. Porcelain Italian tile was used, adding to the luxe, dream-like space.
Photographs by Barkin-Gilman Group

ACTWO Architects, page 383

Saniee Architects, pag

JMKA | architects, pag

NORTHEASTERN US

BELOW & FACING PAGE: The house is a long, goldenrod-colored, and mahogany box that floats above a structured field at the edge of a grove of trees. The sheltering, mahogany lined entry is under a dramatic cantilever that has a number of dramatic openings to the sky and the grove of trees to the south.
Photographs by Greg Premru

ACTWO Architects

In designing houses and living environments, ACTWO Architects works to inspire and innovate in the creation of transformative spaces that are a pleasure to inhabit. ACTWO is a collaborative group of architects, led by Thomas White and Andrew Cohen, who work together with the entire office on all aspects of the residential projects that the firm undertakes, from small houses or condominiums to larger residences on significant sites. The work reflects the creativity of the company's employees, with each project representing the input of the full team in a cooperative approach to design.

Their inspiration derives from the idea of the modern house, which privileges spatial experiences over conventionally designed, programmatic elements. Spatial interaction and volumetric continuity become protagonists in an ongoing experiential conversation within the living spaces. The interrelationship between inside and outside becomes paramount in extending the house's impact into its environment. The expression of natural materials and the clarity of the overall forms are part of the lexicon of expression that make up the projects that they are most proud of, and creates a visual continuity that allows for different stylistic outcomes within an overall clear intention.

BELOW: Strategic cuts in the overall volume of the upper floor mass allow light to penetrate deep into the interior of the house in unexpected places. The garage is underneath, with a custom hydraulic polycarbonate and aluminum single door discreetly placed in the recessed ground floor plane. The kitchen door exits to an outdoor eating area adjacent to the modern parterres of the garden.

FACING PAGE TOP: The entry connects to a dynamic stair that floats in a volume that ties the lower-level living spaces to the private rooms above.

FACING PAGE BELOW: A path of metallic tile extends from the stair through the living room to a dramatic sculpted landscape beyond. The floor-to-ceiling windows further extend the continuity of the living space into the exterior environment.
Photographs by Greg Premru

ABOVE: The simple, compact form of the house is inflected by the angled recess articulating the front door. The vertical cedar siding references the vertical reading of the trees beyond.

LEFT: The house is positioned directly along the edge of a heavily wooded slope. The deck extends the ground plane of the front lawn and overlooks the wooded site.

FACING PAGE TOP: The kitchen is the primary space of the house, with the utility functions located beneath the bridge connecting the upper-level bedrooms and the two-story windows affording tree-canopy-level views of the woods.

FACING PAGE BOTTOM: The open floor plan is organized around the mass of the fireplace and main stair connecting all three levels.
Photographs by Greg Premru

"We use form and materiality to define living space. This frames the exterior environment, allowing nature to be absorbed into the architecture."
—ACTWO Architects

BELOW: The house is organized around the outdoor living space with large doors that open fully to connect the interior with the exterior. Large window screens are concealed in pockets along the edge of the openings. Linear garden spaces articulate this transition between inside and outside.

FACING PAGE TOP: The simple form of the kitchen opens directly to the breakfast area and den beyond. The cooktop is illuminated by a linear skylight above.

FACING PAGE CENTER: The dining and living area opens to the outdoor living space beyond.

FACING PAGE BOTTOM: The large exterior opening is located to allow daylight to fully illuminate the living area interior.
Photographs by Myroslav Rosky

BELOW & FACING PAGE: This shore property was built to minimize maintenance and uses cement board, cellular PVC, and natural cedar on the exterior. We used the wood at steps and entrances in particular—emphasizing the visual beauty and tactile warmth that the material offers. Placements of bold white elements add a modern edge to this home set within an historic seaside community.
Photographs by Paul S. Bartholomew Photography, LLC

Always by Design

The idea of tranquil asymmetry may seem improbable, but after studying the work of Ed Barnhart, it's obvious that this is not only possible, but highly appealing. He finds a balance between calm, soothing environments and dynamic elements that will engage the imagination and sustain interest. Here, peace meets art. A wide range of inspirations also find their way into the houses of Always by Design, culled from Ed's extensive international study, work, and travel experiences. The discussion of a single feature, such as a shower, will invariably invite comparisons with Scandinavian, Japanese, and Balinese bathing traditions and aesthetic sensibilities. Ed's profound love of engaging all of one's senses is evidenced by his nuanced selections of materials and handling of natural light.

Coupled with his extensive experience and design sensibilities is a strong hands-on approach. Ed engages completely with every project. No detail is minor and every decision matters. The idea of total engagement extends itself to the homeowners, as well. Ed encourages them to ask questions and stay closely involved. After having designed and renovated his own family homes over the years, Ed is empathetic to the homeowners' needs, as well as their essential role in the building process. By remaining involved, the homeowners will know their new residence intimately and bond with it even before they move in. That's the ultimate reward of Ed's architectural practice.

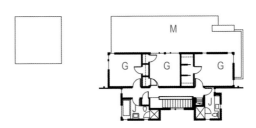

SECOND FLOOR PLAN

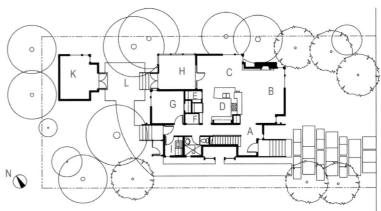

N

FIRST FLOOR PLAN

A – Foyer	H – Screened Porch
B – Living Room	I – Laundry
C – Dining Room	J – Bathroom
D – Kitchen	K – Studio
E – Pantry	L – Deck
F – Mechanical	M – Vegetative Roof
G – Bedroom	

TOP: We wanted to capture a Zen-like serenity in the dining room and did so by using a limited palette, as far as materials and colors are concerned. The doors lead to a screened-in porch with a matching unfinished-cedar ceiling and pergola feel. There is a defined sense of space, even with an open plan.

BOTTOM: Curb-less and open, this Scandinavian-style shower with operable window captures the beauty of an everyday activity. I built the sliding cedar shutter to add flexibility year-round, but particularly to enhance the summer indoor showering experience—enabling daylight and natural breezes to enter—while still maintaining privacy.

FACING PAGE TOP: The white oak floors of the living room utilize wide, solid-wood planks that naturally cup with the changes in humidity of the coastal environment. Particularly for barefoot summer users, this adds an element of naturalness and tactile engagement. The corner windows add a sense of diagonal movement and speak to the waterside feel of the home.

FACING PAGE BOTTOM: Designed for LEED Silver, the home features a harvested-water irrigation system for maintaining discreet lawn play areas and low-water vegetation for the rest of the property—gracefully balancing recreational and ecological objectives.
Photographs by Paul S. Bartholomew Photography, LLC

"Light does more than anything to establish the character of a space and provide joy."
—Ed Barnhart

BELOW & FACING PAGE: Set on 120 acres near the quaint village of Rhinebeck in upstate New York, this single-family home is a modern take on the local, historic barns of the Hudson River Valley and is designed to adapt over time from a weekender to a full-time residence. The house exterior utilizes cladding of plantation softwood treated to manifest hardwood characteristics—it is maintenance-free, unpainted, unstained, insect and mold-resistant, and dimensionally stable. This cladding was applied as a rain-screen to all outside walls and entirely covers the roof, using a unique, innovative clip system atop the standing seams of the metal sheeting underneath—a first for a private home in North America.
Photographs by Oliver Mint

Amalgam Studio

Founded in 2016 by Australian-born Ben Albury, Amalgam Studio aims to produce thoughtful, cohesive, refined, and sustainable built work. The emerging interdisciplinary design firm, based in New York City, blends the realms of architecture, interior, furniture, and product design. Amalgam Studio was recently honored with an invitation to the 2020 ECC Architecture Exhibition, running in conjunction with the Venice Architecture Biennale. This high-profile exhibition showcases the work of 170 selected well-known—and up-and-coming—architectural firms from around the world and will be attended by an estimated 600,000 visitors.

Albury graduated with honors from the University of Melbourne architecture program, before working with award-winning Australian architectural design firms such as LAB, Bates Smart, and John Wardle Architects. After moving to New York City in 2008, he became an Associate Principal at Kohn Pedersen Fox, before moving on to ODA and TFI, creating a body of work across three continents, and specializing in façade documentation, lobby design, and residential interiors. He has over 20 years of diverse, real-world experience across commercial, residential, civic, institutional, mixed-use, hospitality, and interior architecture. In his spare time, he takes freehand drawing commissions at www.bcalbury.com.

BELOW: A study into the local, historic barn types of Dutch, English, and New England heritage informed decisions towards interior planning, overall massing, and the strong gable form. These archetypical barns also inspired the use of exposed structural framework, cathedral ceilings, loft spaces, large sliding glass "barn" doors, natural stone cladding to the basement walls, wood lining to the interiors, and timber cladding to walls and roofing.

FACING PAGE: Ultimately, this is a house that plays with light. Daylighting is harvested through multiple skylights to the loft, while the central skylights over the stairwell span the entire width of the house, separating it into zones of public and private. Tilt-up sunscreen devices create an ever-changing poetic play of sunlight and shadow throughout the day along the entire length of the house's main corridor.
Photographs by Oliver Mint

"*Design is one of those traits that is uniquely human, along with consciousness, tool-making, language, empathy and the abilty to plan for the future.*"
—Ben Albury

BELOW: The 100-foot-long main house structure is made up of fourteen repetitive, charred, prefabricated Douglas Fir "bent frames," which were raised one by one from the horizontal and bolted upright into place. Much like the traditional community barn-raising events of the past, the entire timber structure of the home was raised in one day.
Photograph by Oliver Mint

BELOW TOP: From the very beginning the clients wanted a comfortable house, so the design followed the extremely energy efficient concepts of the German Passive House standards. Specifically, the house employs a high-performance façade of super-insulation, air-tight membranes, ventilated rain screens, and triple glazing throughout. Adjustable exterior sunshading devices and in-wall heat-recovery ventilation units help ensure an adaptable and comfortable interior environment year-round. Operable windows and sliding doors are positioned to encourage cross-ventilation. Picture windows were carefully positioned to enhance and celebrate natural daylight and the ever-changing seasonal scenery and views beyond.

BELOW CENTER: Local materials informed interior finish selections. Tree species endemic to the wooded site were selected for warmth and character: white oak for flooring and lining, walnut for cabinetry, hickory for feature vanity units. Local granite, slate, and domestic quarried marble guided choices for the chimney hearth, wet areas, and master ensuite, respectively.
Photographs by Oliver Mint & Jesse Turnquist

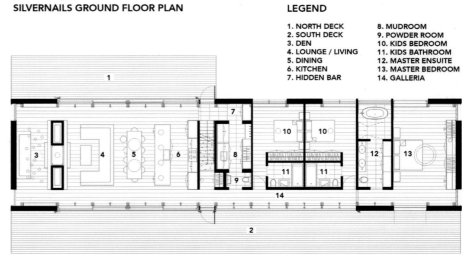

SILVERNAILS GROUND FLOOR PLAN

LEGEND

1. NORTH DECK
2. SOUTH DECK
3. DEN
4. LOUNGE / LIVING
5. DINING
6. KITCHEN
7. HIDDEN BAR
8. MUDROOM
9. POWDER ROOM
10. KIDS BEDROOM
11. KIDS BATHROOM
12. MASTER ENSUITE
13. MASTER BEDROOM
14. GALLERIA

BELOW: We designed the Chilmark Meadow Residence for a collector of Frank Lloyd Wright, so we focused on craftsmanship and organic connection to the natural landscape at the exterior of the home. We implemented low-profile roof lines and natural materials including wood, granite, glass, and metal. Adjacent to the front entrance is the artist's studio where we added clerestory windows to bring in natural indirect light from all four directions during all seasons.

FACING PAGE: Both the design and outdoor spaces were crafted to capture views of important existing site features, including a 200-year-old, hand-built stone wall, an expansive meadow, a glacial boulder, a vernal pond, and a small grove of apple trees.
Builder: Baumhofer Estes, Inc.
Photographs by Wayne Smith

Architecture + Indigo

Founding principal of Architecture + Indigo, Debra Cedeno is often referred to as "old-school" because she can still be found drawing by hand to demonstrate preliminary design concepts and details. While this drawing method has more or less become obsolete; her use of this artistic rendering tool is one reason why the firm is so unique. Creating bespoke drawings enables her and her team to more closely connect with their clients and ultimately to create beautiful buildings.

Architecture + Indigo specializes in residential architecture and is committed to promoting excellence in design that truly illustrates their passion for their work. Debra maintains close client communication throughout the design process and is involved in every aspect of the project. Her solutions to design challenges are innovative and distinctive, and the firm's personalized approach is key to efficiently and successfully translating the architectural vision into the completed home.

Architecture + Indigo understands that designing a home is a lasting and important collaboration and they pay close attention to every detail. As year-round residents of Martha's Vineyard, the firm offers expertise about the island and focus their work on comfortable and efficient floor plans that take advantage of the sunshine and the beautiful landscape. Ultimately, they craft each home for harmonious enjoyment by family and friends.

BELOW TOP: We carried key design details throughout the Chilmark house, including the stone piers and walls that anchor the structure; the piers are battered on three sides to accentuate the supportive nature of stone. Other signature elements repeated throughout are the mitered corner and clerestory windows and the low-pitch profile of the "razor edge roof" that appears to float. We also eliminated all window and door trim on both the interior and the exterior, celebrating simplicity and an efficient connection without decoration.
Photograph by Wayne Smith

BELOW BOTTOM: The design of the interior spaces fosters a sense of calm by utilizing natural materials that are joined with clean details as well as comfortably proportioned spaces.
Photograph by Michael Partenio

"An affinity to the use of simple forms and natural materials in symphony with a thoughtful connection to the landscape creates impactful results."
—Debra Cedeno

BELOW TOP: The living room's stone fireplace, with its floating stone hearth, is a pivotal design element of the house from both the exterior and the interior; it denotes the central gathering space. Every window is strategically focused on a landscape feature and almost every room of the house has a door that directly leads to a meadow, a terrace, or a garden.

BELOW BOTTOM LEFT: The floor plan is organized into three areas, including this entertaining-friendly dining space that flows seamlessly into the living room.

BELOW BOTTOM RIGHT: We designed the kitchen as a place for the family to share in meal preparation and for guests to linger while enjoying dining together in an abundantly sunlit space. The stone veneer columns evoke the same feeling of the exterior, directly connecting to the landscape and views.
Photographs by Michael Partenio

"Modern architecture can be expressed through the careful and innovative integration of wood, glass, stone and metal—all with clean lines and the absence of ornament."
—Debra Cedeno

ABOVE: This Modern Farmhouse is nestled on a heavily wooded lot with close proximity to the ocean, nature paths, and a fresh water pond. Therefore, we designed the home to easily support indoor and outdoor entertaining for the owners and their guests with elevated decks and covered, screened porches. Private bedroom wings feature windows on all four sides, and the master suite and guest room connect to the center gathering space by means of floor-to-ceiling glass connectors that offer a unique source of natural light to mark the transition from one space to the next.
Photograph by Wayne Smith

LEFT: The exposed rafters on the covered front porch along with the painted clapboard and swing reference classic farmhouse details, offering a unique juxtaposition to the modern glass connector that marks the transition to a different part of the house. The brilliant-blue entry door is a thoughtful reference to the owner's family history.

FACING PAGE TOP: The central gathering space has cathedral ceilings, scaled down by the use of natural wood collar ties and warm materials that are echoed in the fireplace mantle and all three exterior doors. The large expanse of glass in the main living space provides a true connection to the adjacent woods, which was a very important design feature for the homeowners.

FACING PAGE BOTTOM: The kitchen incorporates clean lines and optimizes natural sunlight—and we used continuous open, floating shelves for both a functional and poetic effect. A screened porch dining area and lounge are conveniently located next to the kitchen and serve as a natural overflow for guests in any weather.
Builder: Laurence Clancy Construction, Inc.
Interior Designer: Tracey Overbeck Stead
Photographs by Ethan Stead

BELOW & FACING PAGE: Trail side at Killington, Vermont's largest ski area, Lift House captures the panoramic views of the Green Mountains. The expressive three-story form is clad in corten steel and cedar. The upper cantilevered cedar roof and deck structure floats above the ground visually, tying the architecture to the landscape. The house sits integrated into the backslope of the site. A two-story glass wall accentuates the entry foyer's custom steel staircase.
Photographs by Erica Allen Studio

Birdseye

Birdseye began in 1984 as a small building company rooted in the craft of custom residential construction. The firm has since developed into an employee-owned, award-winning architecture and building collaborative that continues the pursuit of artistry in both design and building. Birdseye employs skilled craftspeople, including architects, builders, wood workers, metal workers, and excavation machine operators who prioritize refinement and creativity in each project. Bringing together innovation and tradition, Birdseye aims to create unique homes that inspire.

Principal architect Brian Mac, FAIA, draws inspiration from a variety of places: art, music, nature, architecture, and the collaborative process. He encourages clients to both trust and challenge the team throughout each phase of design and construction. This interaction fosters creativity and nets authentic results.

Maintaining the highest standards of design for each project, the firm practices a regionalist approach to each concept. Birdseye creates contemporary expressions of architecture inspired by the vernacular landscape. Every project is a continued effort of conceptual refinement. Because each building is unique in context and client, the designs express exclusive aspects that are drawn from a diverse set of circumstances, ultimately connecting both the landscape and homeowner to a bespoke design.

Basement Floor Plan

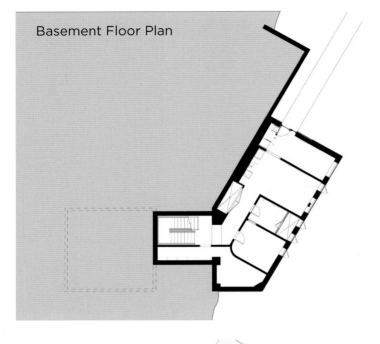

First Floor Plan

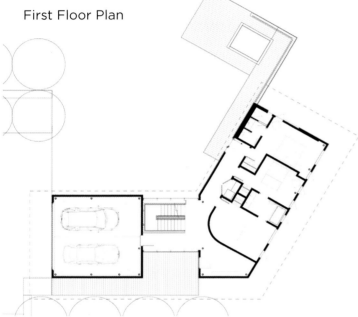

"Scale is a critical element in a room. It sets the tone for the experience."
—Brian Mac, FAIA

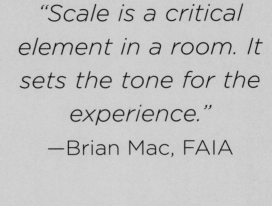

Second Floor Plan

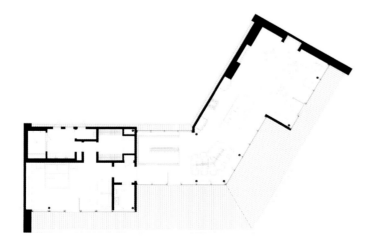

FACING PAGE TOP LEFT: The open floor plan is anchored with a wood-burning fireplace in the main entertainment space. We wanted to emphasize the surrounding natural beauty and refrain from blocking any sightlines, so the continuous panoramic view is seen through the floor-to-ceiling glass wall composition.

FACING PAGE TOP RIGHT: Strengthened through the continuity of materials on the ceiling and floor, the open floor plan shows off the simple, stunning aesthetic of the elements used to create the home. All upper-floor spaces flow out to the exterior porch space.

FACING PAGE BELOW: We accentuated the indoor-outdoor relationship with the exterior open porch. The large, cantilevered roof and deck highlight the provocative form and provide an inspiring view to the Vermont landscape.
Photographs by Erica Allen Studio

BELOW & FACING PAGE: The house is sited on a ridge 200 feet above the Potomac River in McLean, Virginia, much closer to the water than the previous 1970s-era home was. Appearing to be single-story from the street front, the stucco-clad structure is revealed from the river side to be three levels, all glass-walled to showcase the view. Vaulted roofs evoke airplane hangars and Roman forms, echoing both the homeowner's line of work and classic design. Balconies also run the length of the home, providing even more access to the extraordinary river views from this two-plus-acre site.
Photographs by Gordon Beall

Christian Zapatka Architect

Seeking to fuse the best of both modern and traditional design in order to create classic, timeless structures, the award-winning Christian Zapatka Architect designs new houses as well as additions to and renovations of existing houses. Founded in 2001, the firm has completed over 100 projects in the Washington, D.C. area. Only three years after its founding, the firm was one of five winners in the AIA Rowhouse of the Future Competition. More recently, Christian and his team were invited to participate in the History Channel's Future Cities Competition, presenting their work at Washington's Union Station. The firm's work has been featured in numerous publications, including *Home & Design's* (DC/MD/VA) portfolio of top designers. Christian has also recently served as a juror for the Palladio Awards.

A member of the American Institute of Architects and a Fellow of The American Academy in Rome, Christian earned his master's degree in architecture from Princeton University. While there, he was awarded the Norton Prize for excellence in design and then apprenticed for two years with Michael Graves. In 1991, he was awarded the Rome Prize in architecture to spend a year in residence at the American Academy in Rome. Zapatka also taught architectural design and history for seven years at Princeton, Columbia, and the University of Michigan. He has authored two books, with *The American Landscape* being awarded an AIA International Book Award in 1998. Zapatka is a member of the Committee of 100 on the Federal City and a member of the Cosmos Club in Washington, D.C.

BELOW & FACING PAGE: While the house is mostly open-plan, there is one element that cleverly separates the public areas: the "central core." This houses service and circulation, including a shaft for a future elevator and the chimney for the living room fireplace on the outer face of the core. The wood block, glass, and steel staircase is set against the inner face of the core, leading up to the second-floor office and down to the exercise room and guest suite. The central vaulted roof stretches over the stairwell with its surrounding catwalk as well as the office and its porch overlooking the river.
Photographs by Gordon Beall

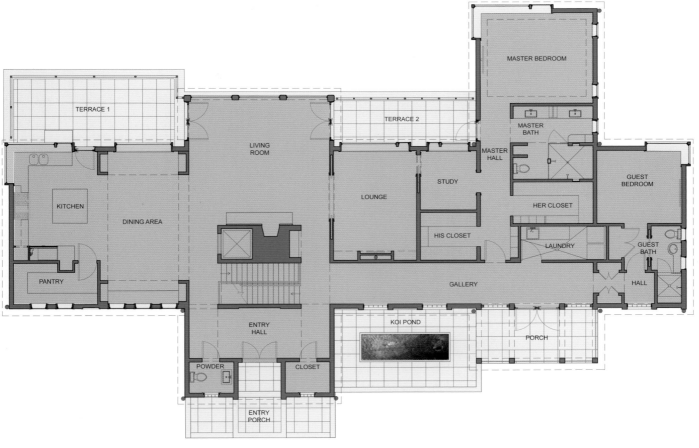

FIRST FLOOR PLAN

2013   PRIVATE RESIDENCE
McLEAN, VIRGINIA

BELOW & FACING PAGE: We built the Garrison House on a dramatic cliff overlooking the Hudson River. This "green" house and garden features a planted meadow roof, corner windows to capture views of Bear Mountain and down river, and an enclosed entry rock garden. The main floor features an open living-dining-kitchen area anchored by a stone fireplace, the master bedroom, and a separate guest cottage/music room. We used cedar, steel, glass, and stone. The tower houses a home office and an upper deck with views to West Point.
Photographs by Elliott Kaufman

Gertler & Wente Architects

Gertler & Wente Architects is a Manhattan-based mid-size firm committed to exploring the intersection of modernism and contextual/regional residential design. Their design approach incorporates a rigorous response to a client's aspirations, the site, sun orientation, history, and sustainability. Founded in 1985, the firm offers a variety of services including architectural, garden, and interior design. Gertler & Wente Architects is well-versed in a variety of styles, but always executes with a careful attention to detail and a deep connection to the environment.

Larry J. Wente, AIA, LEED AP, has known that he wanted to be an architect since age 11. He spent much of his youth drawing, painting, and designing homes. He still carries that same passion and, today, runs the firm with Jeffrey J. Gertler, AIA. They develop a deep relationship with homeowners, including having every client complete a preliminary questionnaire that asks them to describe important place memories and abstract ideas related to their dream home. It's an effective way to glean insight and allows them to translate a homeowner's aspiration into built form.

BELOW TOP: The Ulster County House is set within a 200-plus-acre water park near the Hudson River. We designed it to capture south and western views of various spring-fed, interconnecting ponds and their surrounding mature gardens filled with native grasses, perennials, and specimen trees. The master bedroom suite is housed in its own wing facing south and east toward a dramatic waterfall feeding the primary pond. We designed the garden surrounding the house.

BELOW BOTTOM: The discreet entry is housed in a stone cube—quarried from the site— and offers an intimately-scaled art-filled space with a framed view of the expansive landscape to the south.
Photographs by Elliott Kaufman

"Our approach is modern, but firmly rooted in the architectural context of the area."
—Larry J. Wente

BELOW TOP: A large chef's kitchen was designed to be open to the sun room and includes stainless steel appliances, soapstone counters, and hand-lacquered custom cabinetry. Our client really cooks—creating fantastic multiple-course meals that are locally sourced and beautifully presented.

BELOW BOTTOM: The owner's extensive art collection was carefully designed into the residence as was the art and landscape lighting. Materials include wide-plank rift-cut oak floors, plaster walls, and full-slab bathrooms. The mechanics of heating and cooling are generated through a geo-thermal field and geo-thermal pumps.
Photographs by Elliott Kaufman

BELOW: Located in a clearing in the woods with expansive views to the Southern Berkshire Hills, the Sharon Connecticut House was designed to accommodate an active retired couple and the frequent visits of their extended family. It's set on a quarter-mile wooded drive that ends in a defined forecourt, anchored by a barn-red clapboard entrance pavilion set against Connecticut limestone and natural cedar walls. From the entrance, you step into the living room with a 36-foot-long window wall capturing the distant views. A blind-mortared limestone double-sided fireplace divides the living and dining spaces. We were also responsible for the interior design and the structure of the surrounding landscape. Sustainable features include FSC-certified wood throughout, a five-kilowatt solar array, closed-cell insulation, radiant heat, and passive cooling.
Photographs by Elliott Kaufman

BELOW TOP: The kitchen takes advantage of long-distance views of the Housatonic Valley and includes shaker-style custom cherry cabinets, granite and butcher-block counters, and high-end stainless steel appliances.

BELOW BOTTOM: The open plan is based on a four-by-four-foot module as well as proportions based on the golden section. The main level includes the entry, living, dining, kitchen, sun room, study, and master bedroom suite. A contained vegetable and herb garden is located between the two-car garage and the kitchen. The lower level includes three additional bedrooms, a ping-pong room, and a bunk room for grandchildren.
Photographs by Elliott Kaufman

"The quality of light brought into spaces is the key to our architecture."
—Larry J. Wente

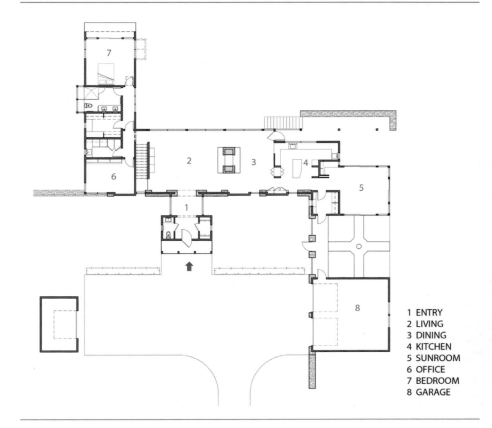

1 ENTRY
2 LIVING
3 DINING
4 KITCHEN
5 SUNROOM
6 OFFICE
7 BEDROOM
8 GARAGE

BELOW: When we designed the Long Dune Residence in Truro, Massachusetts, we wanted it to respond to three distinct views: primarily the Atlantic Ocean, but also the Pamet River and a nearby fresh-water pond. The home is perched on a coastal bluff in the Cape Cod National Seashore Park, and was built to withstand the rough weather. The house is clad in western red cedar and mahogany that will age to a natural soft gray and blend into the natural wooded landscape.

FACING PAGE: The entry side of the house presents a solid and private appearance, with thick, super-insulated wood-clad walls and narrow strip windows enclosing bathrooms, outdoor showers, the laundry room, and other private spaces. Little of the view on the Atlantic facing side is revealed until entering the house through a full-height glass door, which is evident as you approach the house.
Photographs by Peter Vanderwarker

Hammer Architects

Hammer Architects' designs are informed by a tradition of modern homes, particularly the ones created by European architects who emigrated to the U.S. and designed houses on Cape Cod before the 1950s. You can see this in the firm's sensitivity to homes' surroundings, the use of natural light, and the incorporation of environmental elements. Principals Mark Hammer and Don DiRocco make up the firm leadership. A strong respect for context is critical to their design approach.

With two Massachusetts locations—one in Cambridge and one in Truro—Hammer Architects maintains close collaborative relationships and provides substantial principal involvement in all phases of a project. They offer innovative solutions to suit an array of budgets, schedules, and program objectives. Both architects have impressive backgrounds. Mark has worked in the industry for more than 40 years and has been a part of awarding-winning projects like the US Navy Submarine Museum in Groton, Connecticut. Don has experience with a number of Boston-area firms. He joined Hammer Architects in 2008 and advanced to become a principal in 2018. Their extensive knowledge allows them to discover creative ways to meet and exceed homeowners' expectations.

BELOW TOP: We designed the screened porch with a referential diamond, kite-shaped roof that acts as a hinge which occupies the intersection of the two geometries. It provides additional views in several directions and enhances the natural airflow through the home.

BELOW BOTTOM: Because the homeowners plan to retire here, the house was created for one-level living. The long south wing encloses the guest bedrooms and a home office. The north wing, which is rotated 45 degrees in plan and oriented to the verdant view of the Pamet River, houses the master bedroom suite.

FACING PAGE TOP & BOTTOM: Natural light and air flow were key elements for this house. This is apparent in the use of large, functional windows in every space. Deep roof overhangs with ventilating clerestory windows promote natural cooling and ventilation while shading the interior in the summer months. We additionally used passive and active solar design principles and incorporated photovoltaic panels at the garage roof.
Photographs by Peter Vanderwarker

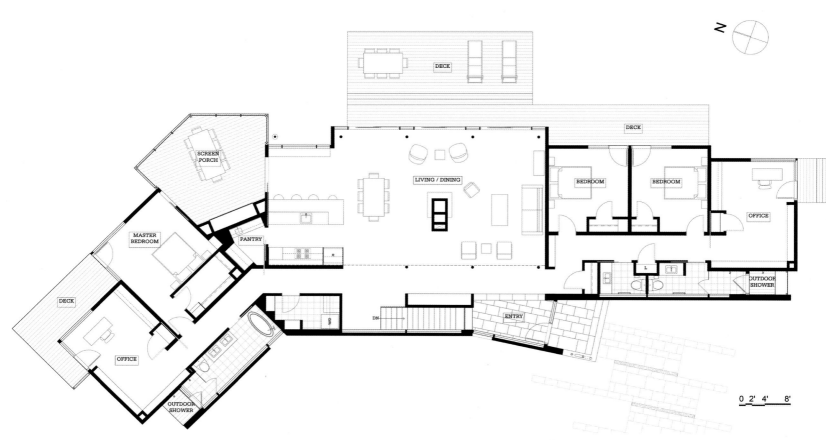

"*Discovery is the first step of design. We listen to our clients, spend time on the site, and connect with the natural environment.*"

—Mark Hammer

BELOW: Inspired by the spirit of Texas Hill Country homes—even though this property is far from Texas—we designed this expansive residence around a sprawling courtyard.

FACING PAGE: The property is partly bordered by a park, affording both privacy and a lush natural environment.
Photographs courtesy of Harpole Architects

Harpole Architects

A passion for architecture and interior design has always driven Jerry Harpole to produce work that provides a context-derived and special place for each of his clients. To that end, he founded Harpole Architects in 1987 and has been focusing on custom, high-end residential projects ever since.

He believes that architecture and interior design are inextricably linked, so he does both—and well. That's just one of the reasons his clients keep returning to him for second, maybe even third or fourth, homes.

Whether it's an 18th century Georgian design or a 21st century modern, Jerry adapts an appropriate style that's desirable to the homeowner and responsive to the environment. Indeed, it's the variety that really keeps him interested with inspiration coming from just about everywhere, including travel and the time he spent studying at the École des Beaux-Arts in Paris, France.

When it comes to his design process, though, he will admit to being more traditional; a "little bit of a dinosaur." But, in this case, that's a very good thing—meaning, he creates compelling design sketches by hand for each of his projects. "Hand drawings give a mood; they seduce the client," he says. "It's a different experience than what CAD provides; sometimes computers just don't cut it."

Drawings aside, for Jerry, the most important element of a distinctive and exceptional design is not so much the style, but how a home and each of its rooms makes someone feel.

BELOW TOP: The central, three-sided courtyard, which is not visible from the street, reveals itself as you walk through the house; there is a bit of mystery as it unfolds.

BELOW BOTTOM: Using both stucco and Texas limestone for the exterior in addition to the copper and faux slate roof is at once rustic and refined.

FACING PAGE: We collaborated with Jeff Plusen of Plusen Landscape Architects to create the comfortably modern tone of the courtyard landscaping.
Photographs courtesy of Harpole Architects

BELOW: This renovation of a house on 200 acres in Napa, California is the epitome of wine country sophistication. In the living and dining area, the vaulted wood ceilings and sleek furnishings, paired with the homeowner's incredible art collection, provide a rustic-modern aesthetic.

FACING PAGE TOP: For this condominium in Washington, D.C., the client was interested in expressing peace and harmony through design. So, we offered a respite from the city with a tranquil, organic space that felt connected to nature in spite of its industrial elements.

FACING PAGE BOTTOM: We love this custom master suite, most of all of for its floating statement ceiling. The panels of dark-veined pine are a dramatic counterpoint to the neutral tones of the room.
Photographs courtesy of Harpole Architects

"With wit and passion for architecture and interior design, we express each client's specific desires for a distinctive and exceptional place."
—Jerry Harpole

JMKA | architects

When it comes to residential architecture, principal and lead designer Jeff Kaufman believes that close collaboration is the best approach. His tight-knit team at JMKA | architects offers homeowners a personal experience with exactly the right amount of hand holding—because clients should never feel lost or overwhelmed during the process, but instead focused on giving creative and practical insight. Here, homeowners are always informed, involved, and engaged with consultants, specialists, and members of the JMKA team throughout the project.

Because a custom home is an extension of its site, material selection is important. Always mindful of the environment, Jeff and his team source local materials where possible and opt for sustainable, timeless solutions. The idea is for the house to merge with and respect its landscape—authenticity is key.

Travel is also an influential design factor for Jeff and his team, and informs much of the firm's work. Although he has been an architect for more than 15 years in Westport, Connecticut, Jeff travels extensively. With no one style, the firm's designs have gained attention outside of Connecticut. JMKA | architects has projects in Massachusetts, Maine, Vermont, Florida, and Georgia.

ABOVE & LEFT: Initially, the entry courtyard was dark and closed off. To open it up and let in the natural light, we created a glass cube-like structure that rises above the roof and allows light to pass through the lush vegetation. It keeps the space bright and vibrant without obstructing views of the greenery.

FACING PAGE TOP: This house has distinct rounded walls, and we wanted to maintain those lines wherever possible during the renovation. But because the homeowner is an avid art lover, we wanted to ensure that he could also display his collection, and the living room allows for that. You will see recurring design details here: The woodwork on the bookcase mimics that of the home's exterior.

FACING PAGE BOTTOM: To maintain the integrity of the home's shape, we expanded the master bathroom without altering the exterior. The new space does not extend beyond the depth of the eaves. In the kitchen, we kept the cylindrical shape of the room and used African Sapele mahogany for the cabinets—the same wood that is found in the rest of the home.
Photographs by David Heald Photography

"Good materials do not go out of style. We create a timeless design that will appeal to multiple generations."
—Jeff Kaufman

BELOW: A series of design decisions responded to the impact of climate change on the coast. The fact that Mother Nature is in control led us to design defensively by raising the house 10 feet on piers, with hurricane-resistant openings. Nature is a major character in this production—after all, this house replaces one that succumbed to Hurricane Sandy.

FACING PAGE: The house's organization can be reduced to a few sweeping gestures coalescing around the notion of two joined structures: the house and the porch. The porch is elevated to a co-equal status, providing a protected southeast view to the bay of which all rooms share.
Photographs by Don Paine

KGP design studio

Residential buildings might be a small portion of KGP Design Studio's portfolio—the award-winning firm mostly focuses on civic and infrastructure structures—but no matter the project, Don Paine and his team are careful to balance private and public spaces. This deep-seated behavioral instinct for "refuge and promontory" is a theme throughout all of KGP's work, as is the idea that architecture is an experience, not an object. For example, a well-designed residential porch not only passively enhances the conditioning and natural lighting of an interior space, but enhances an occupant's interactions with their surroundings, be they an ocean view or a friendly neighbor.

This pragmatic and performance-based—rather than style-driven—approach places a high demand on innovation, often with exciting outcomes in the application of materials, fabrication, and their uses. It emphasizes architecture as a series of mailable transitions that define how we experience the physical or social realm. How its buildings relate to the environment is also a priority for KGP, which acknowledges an overwhelming obligation to ensure that a project is a sustainable contribution to the built environment and enables, or better yet, motivates its users to live a sustainable lifestyle.

BELOW TOP: Where the living level does meet the bay level, nothing is spared. The entry stairs are integrated into what is effectively a grand, cedar-planked amphitheater, turning entering and exiting into a leisurely pastime.

BELOW BOTTOM: Here the porch is an extremely practical and efficient means of tempering the harsh sun and weather conditions on the island, but perhaps more importantly, it is a habitable interlayer: blurring the distinction while framing the transition between inside and outside.
Photographs by Don Paine

BELOW TOP: If the house is a practical defense tuned to the elements, transiently it is a spiritual connection to them; a means of sensitizing and connecting the occupant to his surroundings, and to the changing mood of the bay.

BELOW BOTTOM: This house expresses its tenuous relationship to the ground. The bay-front landscape flows beneath and among the piers, providing exterior room for amenities such as a covered seating, a pool-front kitchen and bar, and a changing/shower room.
Photographs by Don Paine

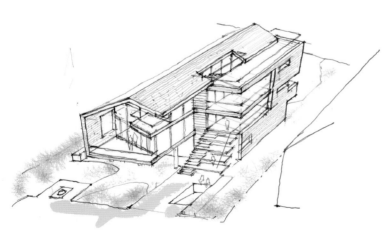

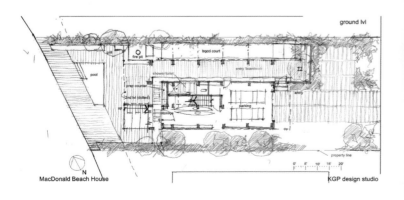

MacDonald Beach House

KGP design studio

BELOW: The rear addition to the architect's own 1950 mid-century modern house, designed by Charles Goodman, is set half a level up the natural slope of the site and is separated from the existing house by a courtyard. We wanted to utilize the same basic tenets of Goodman's architecture, including large expanses of glass, exposed structural elements, and an indoor-outdoor relationship. The new structure includes a den, office, and kids' hangout space with two full bathrooms and a laundry room. Overall, this "Dual Modern" house is intended to operate for a family with a young child, with flow between spaces and sliding walls that allow for future flexibility and change of use.
Photograph by Anice Hoachlander

FACING PAGE: Two shed-roofed volumes flank a central walkway that connects the new addition to the existing house; the walkway serves as a gallery for art display on the lower level and widens to a seating area on the upper level. A "landscape wall" defines this space from the outside.
Photograph by Julia Heine

KUBE architecture

KUBE architecture is a modern architecture studio that challenges the norms of daily life, attempting to reinterpret the ways of working and living in the built environment. Formed in 2005 by Janet Bloomberg and Richard Loosle-Ortega, the studio prioritizes a balance between richness, simplicity, and clean lines, with an emphasis on color, textures, and clearly expressed materials. Both Janet and Richard have traveled extensively in Europe, South America, and South Asia, and their minimal, yet warm, design style has been greatly influenced by these travels.

Not only does KUBE bring fresh modernism to Washington, D.C., they ask their clients to look at their environment in a new way. So, it's no surprise that the use of sustainable materials and building systems is integral to all of the studio's projects, as is educating their clients about the importance of building "green." KUBE celebrates both the critical need for sustainability in general as well as the design opportunities that new green materials offer.

As a boutique firm, KUBE is able to extend to its clients close, personal attention. The partners are involved in every project, regardless of size—from initial design conception to client occupancy and beyond. KUBE maintains that design excellence should be accessible to all clients no matter the budget constraints.

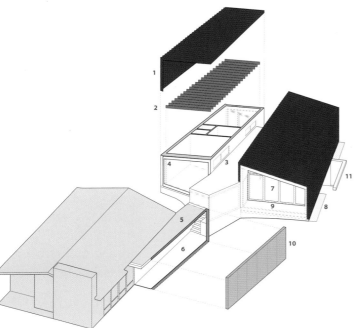

1 Aluminum standing seam roof	**7** Sliding glass wall
2 Exposed wood rafters	**8** Gravel trough
3 Clerestory windows	**9** Porch
4 Exposed steel frame	**10** Landscape wall
5 Green roof	**11** Basement access
6 Gallery	

TOP LEFT: Sliding doors that pocket into the walls join the central walkway to the surrounding spaces in the "dual modern" addition.

TOP RIGHT: We were able to feature clerestory windows in all the rooms of the addition, thanks to the pitch of the shed roofs. These windows offer views of the many trees on site, all of which were preserved during construction. Each room also has a wall of full-height glass on the end, and both ends of the central walkway are glass—all serving to make the landscape the main focal point.

LEFT: This diagram of the "dual modern" addition shows how we put it all together. Metal roofing wraps down the side walls of the new structure, draining water to linear gravel troughs along the perimeter. So, no downspouts or gutters are needed, in effect streamlining the exterior design.
Photographs by Julia Heine

FACING PAGE LEFT: The owners of this traditional Washington row house desired a space of openness and light: "un petit bijou." Our challenge was to completely transform the narrow, dark building—with almost no natural light—into a modern, light-filled space; a "see-through" house. LED lighting lines the perimeter of the glass openings, so they glow at night. In addition to sustainable systems, green materials include bamboo flooring and no-VOC paint.

FACING PAGE TOP RIGHT: In order to achieve this transformation, we established a simple floor plan with no dividing walls and all programmatic elements running along the party walls. Glass floors are aligned on every level as a transparent "volume of light," piercing the roof and creating a tapestry of solid and void inside the house. Floor plates allow light and views to run vertically unobstructed throughout the house.

FACING PAGE BOTTOM RIGHT: Large glass openings provide a vast amount of natural light—there is very little need for artificial light sources, aside from the LEDs.
Photographs by Greg Powers Photography

"We consider every new challenge in the most creative way possible."
—Richard Loosle-Ortega

BELOW: The Oaks, a property within an ancient oak grove on Martha's Vineyard, wraps an existing hilltop knoll rather than sitting atop it. This view of the house from the deck captures the roof layers, which create clerestories between them to bring in the light from above. We implemented untreated cedar shiplap siding, so it will weather to gray and match the natural textures of the woods.

FACING PAGE: The rich and layered nature of the structure unfolds in the dining area and kitchen, where the stone floor and the overhang extends from outside to inside to blur the boundary between the two. By using exterior materials and columns indoors, we created an additional element of ambiguity.
Photographs by Chuck Choi

Maryann Thompson Architects

Recognized by the American Institute of Architects for work that "reconnects architecture with the landscape and celebrates tectonics, materials, and a poetic approach to design," Maryann Thompson, principal at Maryann Thompson Architects, specializes in holistically imagined projects that evoke a rich, sensorial experience while creating a thoughtful edge between interior and exterior space.

With degrees in both architecture and landscape architecture, she is uniquely equipped to balance the relationship of land to site, beautifully reflecting the environment by utilizing light as a medium and integrating warm, natural elements into her designs. Her firm excels in sustainable, regionally driven, and site-specific architecture for a diverse range of projects—from large commercial buildings to small-scale residential homes—collaborating with clients to achieve artistically compelling yet functional design solutions.

Her team hails from a variety of professional backgrounds, including landscape architecture, green architecture, planning, interior design, and the visual arts, allowing for carefully considered and dynamically innovative work.

BELOW: The Eagle Meadow House is located among the pastures and old stonewalls of New Hampshire and opens up to the landscape and sun through broad expanses of glass and sliding doors towards the river. An undulating footprint defines a series of outdoor rooms which frame unique views from or through the house to the meadow, river, horizon, and sky.

FACING PAGE TOP: The sliding doors in the kitchen seamlessly open the space to the surrounding landscape.

FACING PAGE CENTER: A folded steel staircase animates the entry.

FACING PAGE BOTTOM: The master suite features a view of the river. The doors of this second-floor bedroom slide open to give the feeling of an old-fashioned sleeping porch.
Photographs by Chuck Choi

"We believe great art, including architecture, should resonate emotionally."
—Maryann Thompson

TOP: The one-story Egret Meadow home on Martha's Vineyard is conceived of carefully placed horizontal planes met by delicate glass walls and doors. The large overhang on the south side shields the expanses of glass from the sun and creates an "extension room" on the deck that overlooks the inlet and meadow beyond.

LEFT: The entry is a "dogtrot;" a southern vernacular that lets the breeze blow through and creates a wonderful transition to the site.

FACING PAGE TOP: In the living room, dining room, and kitchen, we invited the tranquility of the surrounding land to become a part of the space through sliding doors, thus heightening the sense of trust between nature and home while creating ambiguity between the interior and exterior.

FACING PAGE BOTTOM: The interior spaces of the home, including the kitchen, are built around the multiple planes of light entering the rooms at different points during the day. Together, with the light wood and furnishings, the warmth of the natural sunlight creates a peaceful environment.
Photographs by Jeremy Bittermann

BELOW & FACING PAGE: We designed a house for an international couple set in a neighborhood along the Potomac River. As a nod to Moroccan and European heritage, we created a private courtyard-style house with Moroccan roots. A large living space replaced the traditional courtyard and serves as the heart of the home. American aspects include substantial construction, sustainable elements, energy efficiency, and clear organization. Materials include steel, glass, zinc, and concrete—emitting an overall substantial presence.
Photographs by Julia Heine

McInturff Architects

McInturff Architects is a small firm with tremendous experience. The Maryland-based, six-person studio creates modern designs for residential, commercial, and small-scale institutional buildings across the region. It also offers full interior design services, remodeling, space planning, and sustainable design—all carefully tailored to the specific needs of the people who will use the space.

The firm was started by Mark McInturff, FAIA, in 1986, and he has expanded his team over the years to include top talent. Principal Chris Boyd focuses on an ever-expanding regional emphasis on the Eastern Shore and Atlantic Coast, while principal Peter Noonan focuses on the commercial projects, while also keeping his hand in the residential work.

With houses and buildings all over the region and throughout 16 states, the firm has received more than 360 design awards, including three AIA Institute Honor Awards, two for Interior Architecture and one for Urban Design. The team's work has also appeared in numerous publications, including *Home and Design, Annapolis Home Magazine, The Washington Post,* and *Dwell.*

BELOW & FACING PAGE: Sited on a Georgetown bluff overlooking the Potomac River and Francis Scott Key bridge, this house has, arguably, the best view of any house in the city. It has had three owners over the last 20 years, and we have worked with each one of them. For the first owners, we renovated the rear 15 feet of the original 19th century townhouse. We added a new four-story steel-and-glass curtain wall that revealed the view of the river, plus a new kitchen. The second owners took us to the top to create a roof deck that added an outdoor component to take full advantage of the sweeping views. And the third and current owners gutted, reconfigured, and replaced every surface in the interior in the previously unrenovated portion. We created a staircase that enlarged and replaced the original. It connects all levels, both functionally and now, architecturally.
Below top photograph by Julia Heine
Facing page and below bottom photographs by Anice Hoachlander

"Every structure has a DNA and once you establish that, the building designs itself."
—Mark McInturff

451

"For us, home design is more of a process of discovery, and less one of formula."
—Mark McInturff

ABOVE & RIGHT: White cedar shingles and stainless steel were used on the outside of the home, and will weather naturally. There is no exterior paint or stain. Because of the strict guidelines that protect the Chesapeake Bay, all of the design's decks, porches, and terraces, as well as the mechanical systems, are stacked onto the small footprint of the house. The allowable footprint for everything on the site is sized to the lot's previous house—long gone, but excavated, surveyed, and documented. The result is a modern ark-like design with 1,664 square feet of interior space.

FACING PAGE: This home sits in a quiet cove on the Maryland's Eastern Shore, so the idea of porch spaces were important when we designed it. The first floor has an open plan with multiple sliding doors that turn the all-white interior into a porch. A winding stair rises to two stacked bedrooms on the second and third floors and continues to the rooftop pool. The structure is made of cross-braced steel frames that support the weight on the roof; the frames impose themselves, and are celebrated, throughout the plan.
Photographs by Julia Heine

BELOW: Nestled in a Hemlock-Beech forest adjacent to Squam Lake in New Hampshire, the new guest house transforms the property from a simple lakeside retreat into a three-generation family camp.
Photograph by Chuck Choi

FACING PAGE: The guest house's extended decks, continuous soffits, prominent breezeway, and expansive windows and doors connect the interiors to the wooded lakeside landscape.
Photograph by Tom Murdough

Murdough Design

Murdough Design, founded in 2007, is a small, collaborative design studio focused on site-specific and experientially driven residential architecture. Using the site as its main source of inspiration, the team's design solutions are unique responses to the specifics of its context: space, landscape, climate, light, and the place's cultural history. Their thoughtful use of materials and construction inform an architecture that is both of the moment and timeless. Considered choreography of occupants' movement through the architecture and site create an experiential narrative of spaces, views, and other tangible/intangible moments—further linking architecture and the site to the occupants' perception. In creating these intrinsic connections between the site, landscape, and self, Murdough Design attempts to heighten an awareness of place and one's connection to it.

A belief in the process of exploration and discovery is at the core of the team's approach. Never pre-meditated, designs evolve through a learning process: understanding the client, the site, and other factors specific to each project. Design from an experiential standpoint is prioritized and, at the earliest phases of design, emphasis is given to three-dimensional modeling. This collaborative and iterative approach facilitates a successful design dialogue between the architects and clients.

BELOW & FACING PAGE: Morning light fills the central dining area, which is figuratively and literally the pivotal heart in the building's plan. Afternoon sun filters through the veil of lakeside trees, raking across the main living spaces. The guest house comfortably sleeps 10 and provides generous living spaces by incorporating efficient elements such as built-in storage and seating, pocket doors, and lift-and-slide windows and doors. Western red cedar walls and ceilings and American black walnut wide-plank floors provide a subdued interior envelope, which focuses the view outward, prioritizing the wooded landscape. A reverence for the materiality and craft of wood construction implies a connection to the forest beyond the building.
Photographs by Chuck Choi

BELOW TOP, BELOW BOTTOM, & FACING PAGE: Situated on a forested shoreline of an idyllic lake, the dwelling provides the family respite from their city-based and plugged-in lifestyle. The exterior's dark color and reflective surfaces camouflage the building's appearance from the lake, minimizing its visual impact. Common living spaces extend and connect to the outdoors, with a perforated metal catwalk overlooking the living room and lake beyond. Floor plates and the folded roof act as "visors" to direct views and movement.
Photographs by Chuck Choi

"A building should be intrinsically rooted to the site's context: its light, climate, landscape, and history."
—Tom Murdough

BELOW: Set on 60 acres of rolling pastures near the Blue Ridge Mountains of Virginia's Shenandoah Valley, this home appears to float in a sea of grass. We didn't want the home to compete with its surroundings, so we designed it to blend in to the site, using a minimalist design.

FACING PAGE: When you get closer to the home, it becomes a highly articulated box with a level of detail that's initially hard to detect. We used ipe, a Brazilian hardwood, for the home's exterior because of its ability to show off natural weathering. As it ages, the wood takes on an organic, silver sheen.
Photographs by Morgan Howarth

Nahra Design Group

At Nahra Design Group, nothing is forced. The Washington, DC-based firm is a collaborative group of architects and designers who work on projects that range from modern to traditional, and operate under the premise that design should feel natural. Without allegiance to any one style, the team—led by John Nahra—creates what makes sense for the site, and offers an organic appeal. Using the environment as the framework for every home, the architects and designers capitalize on a few key elements: space, light, and surrounding views. The clients' personal details and lifestyles are key, of course, and they often bring an array of ideas. Those are also thoughtfully interpreted into the home. The homeowners become an important part of the team throughout the design-and-build process. Every design begins with a traditional method: sketching. The client's vision is drawn out in multiple ways and then the process of narrowing begins to find exactly what the homeowner wants.

The full-service boutique architecture firm is made up of a core group of architects and interior designers working together in a creative studio setting. John founded the firm in 2010 and has been inspired by his team and clients. For this project in particular, the team sought the counsel of Lavinia Fici Pasquina. The Italian-born architect collaborates with the team and brings innovation and forward-thinking ideas, in addition to her European perspective.

BELOW: The two-bedroom getaway has a public and a private side, with the living and dining space making up the public area. Here, homeowners can welcome visitors, and take in the view—the primary focus of the rooms. We designed with this sweeping vista in mind, and made sure that it wasn't blocked. Even the kitchen cabinets take up minimal space, with large windows on either side, to avoid obstructing the scenery.

FACING PAGE TOP: At night, the retreat has a strong, monolithic quality. This is the private side of the home, facing the mountains. The mountains offer a feeling of protection even though the large windows give exposure.

FACING PAGE CENTER: The bedroom stays true to the overall design of the residence; we used clean lines and capitalized on the outdoor setting. Floor-to-ceiling windows add to the calming effect and allow the surroundings to become part of the room. We made the space so connected with its site that the grass can grow right up to the windows.

FACING PAGE BOTTOM: Because this house doesn't have a lot in the way of square footage, we made sure that every space had an impact, including the bathroom. We used natural light to capture the beauty of the materials and add to the feeling of being outdoors. The shower is daylit from above, letting the sunshine pour in.
Photographs by Morgan Howarth

Paul Lukez Architecture

As a student in Holland, Paul Lukez was drawn to architecture because it could embody art, history, science, math, engineering, and nature—all at once. He also liked that it served people and society, something he explored through the wisdom of his mentor, multidisciplinary artist Koo Stroo. Today, Paul continues to find inspiration from many sources, and even if they're non-architectural, they're always deeply rooted in the site and project circumstances. Natural light is a particular guide, as Paul and his team are endlessly intrigued by how spaces are given life and form by this "universal gift," as he refers to it, "one that calls upon us to use it with poetic intent and human delight in mind."

This interplay of nature and man-made space echoes the process for Paul, which brings together clients, colleagues, builders, and communities to collectively create something that did not exist before. In the end, Paul's designs celebrate the craft of building; how things come together in special ways that not only resolve important technical details and challenges but bring a sense of calm and comfort to the people occupying a space.

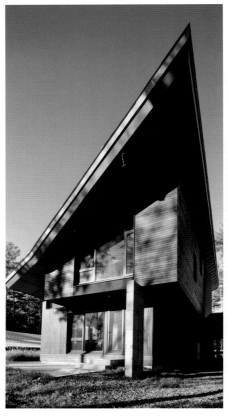

First Floor

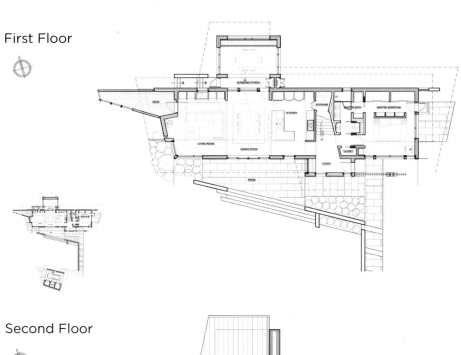

Second Floor

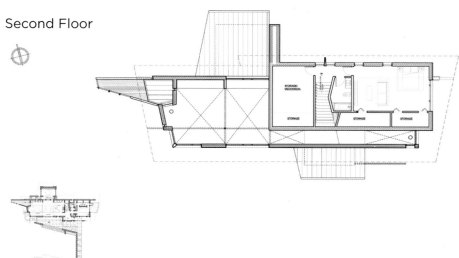

BELOW & FACING PAGE: The south-facing wall's expansive windows flood the interiors with natural light and wintertime heat. Deep roof overhangs prevent overheating in the summertime, while open floor plans and high ceilings enable natural ventilation. In winter, triple-glazed windows, 30-centimeter-thick insulated walls and low-infiltration detailing optimizes heat retention. A wood stove provides supplemental heating.
Photographs by Greg Premru

BELOW & FACING PAGE: While building this waterfront home, we worked with the site's sharply sloped grade elevations and dramatic dropdowns. The design incorporates terraced beds and an infinity pool which are embedded into the landscaping. We kept materials simple and practical. Aluminum tubes make up the pergola, which can withstand humidity and adverse weather. Traditional options, such as wood, are less stable and susceptible to the sometimes-damp coastal climate. The house takes full advantage of solar energy, with solar panels and an orientation that helps it stay warm during the wintertime and cool throughout the summer. We relied on a geothermal system, so no gas or fossil fuels are used.
Photographs by Jon Doucette

S. Barzin Architect

Founded by Shahin Barzin, S. Barzin Architect is an interdisciplinary and design firm based in Rhode Island. Shahin has both a modernist and a preservationist sensibility. He explores new building technologies while respecting historical detail. Shahin is also passionate about sustainable design, incorporating geothermal systems, solar panels, and other innovations into his work. The firm's designs are noted for elegance and practicality, and cover a wide range of residential and commercial products.

Shahin Barzin is also actively engaged in designing domestic and international retail stores as well as designing and developing lines of display furniture and fixtures.

S. Barzin Architect has been a recipient of different awards including the "Preserve Rhode Island Historical Preservation Project Award" for the restoration of Belcourt Mansion in Newport.

Shahin Barzin holds a bachelor's degree from Rhode Island School of Design in both Architecture and Interior Architecture. He is also a member of the American Institute of Architects (AIA) and is certified by the National Council of Architectural Registration Boards (NCARB).

BELOW: We borrow some concepts from my home country, Iran, and in this case, it is the use of water and reflection in the design. Iranian culture often uses water as a key element in architecture; here, the reflection adds a sense of light and another layer of depth to the home.

FACING PAGE TOP & CENTER: We used stonemasonry on the home's exterior, which we transposed into the interior living space. This same strong stone theme appears in the unpaved driveway as well, where we laid turf stone as opposed to a more conventional paved driveway. The turf stones have plenty of space between them and allow grass to grow, adding to the organic quality of the outdoor entrance space.

FACING PAGE BOTTOM: The pool looks out on to the scenic Narragansett Bay and offers the homeowners a space to either relax and reflect, or to entertain.
Photographs by Jon Doucette

"Design is expressed with the understanding that each project is unique in relation to the homeowner's needs and the project's environment."
—Shahin Barzin

BELOW TOP & BOTTOM: We wanted the area around the fireplace to be warm and cozy, so we cantilevered a balcony to close in the space.

FACING PAGE: The homeowner wanted high ceilings, plenty of light, large windows, and an ideal space for uncomplicated furniture and beautiful artwork. Clean and simple, white ash wood appears on the stairs and upper level. We maintained transparency and openness with glass rails on the stairs and balcony.
Photographs by Jon Doucette

BELOW: Updated with elegant lines and gracious design, this Greenwich home provides a fresh take on the quintessential Connecticut farmhouse.

FACING PAGE: This is not your typical farmhouse entry; look up and see laylights which are one of the many ways we implemented upscale technology and creative use of light to transcend the classic concept of a country home.
Photographs by Neil Landino

Saniee Architects

Style is essentially a language for Mahdad Saniee, founder of Saniee Architects; a language in which ideas and content take on a variety of forms and aren't boxed in by any particular aesthetic. That said, he prioritizes timeless elements across his work, partly due to his early training in Scotland where his first jobs were for preservationist architects. He's most inspired by the specific feelings evoked by a place or environment—be it a historic structure, a collective memory, or even a movie set. It is the invention, or the unique recreation, of these sensations that he's most passionate about.

Through this lens, his award-winning architectural service firm designs homes that powerfully resonate with the lives of the people who inhabit them. They collaborate with their clients closely, drawing them into the design process while using scholarship and creativity to shape the outcome.

With a wide variety of residential and institutional projects across the country, Saniee Architects brings a wide range of experience to clients who demand the highest quality and attention to detail along with thorough service. Because they've been so successful in establishing strong, successful relationships, many of their current projects are with repeat clients.

BELOW: In the O'Brien House, we created a sports memorabilia room for the homeowners. But, the hanging beams and the laylights above score just as big when it comes to making a statement.
Photograph by Elliott Kaufman

FACING PAGE TOP LEFT: We wanted the materials, textures, and the colors to do much of the visual architectural work in Lion House. So, we introduced a motif of woven sticks, seen here in the staircase.

FACING PAGE TOP RIGHT: The stick-like motif repeats in the ceiling beams and warm woods to subliminally connect the interior with the exterior in the Lion House living and dining room while low-profile furnishings ensure a modern, sleek finish.

FACING PAGE BOTTOM: The Lion House was inspired by New England farmhouse design—and we upheld that classic vernacular while modernizing its interpretation with an emphasis on seamless glass walls and clean lines. The connectedness between the interior and exterior is beautifully captured in the rear of the home, which opens to the covered porch to extend the living room outdoors.
Photographs by David Sundberg, ESTO

BELOW: This dining room in the modern Tudor home features oak panels and custom plaster medallions that reference classic architecture yet maintain a contemporary finish.

FACING PAGE TOP: At the modern Tudor property, a pool pavilion becomes a sophisticated, second living space—and a beautiful outdoor setting when glimpsed from the main house.

FACING PAGE BOTTOM: Traditional elements of Tudor architecture give the home integrity, as seen from within the pool pavilion here.
Photographs by David Sundberg, ESTO

479

BELOW: Pool houses might typically be left as afterthoughts. But we prioritized this one to create a modern, architectural moment that enchantingly illuminates this heavily wooded property.

BOTTOM LEFT : Two walls of glass at the front and back of the pool house create a sense of transparency to unite the structure with the surrounding environment.

BOTTOM RIGHT: Inside the pool house, automatic glass walls slide open for seamless connection to the water.
Photographs by David Sundberg, ESTO

FACING PAGE: This staircase embodies both reassuring solidity and airy weightlessness for a compelling juxtaposition of form. We wanted it to appear is if the oak treads were floating. The interplay of wood and steel makes abstract reference to a Steinway concert grand piano.
Photograph by Neil Landino

BELOW TOP: This new private outdoor space features a pool and a deck that floats 20 feet about the ground for an intriguing, weightless effect; it's the perfect place to entertain.
Photograph by David Sundberg, ESTO

BELOW BOTTOM: A woven stick ceiling accommodates the structure, lighting, and air distribution and imbues the space with an industrial-modern tone.
Photograph by Neil Landino

"We think of success in terms of how close we have come to making 'places' and not just buildings. The end result should ideally feel inevitable."
—Mahdad Saniee

BELOW TOP: We built this new, high-efficiency modern home from the skeleton of a 1970s spec house.

BELOW BOTTOM: The private court deck seamlessly connects the family room and kitchen as well as the bedrooms and the master suite.
Photographs by David Sundberg, ESTO

BELOW: The residence sits on an unconventional, pie-shaped site with a wide front. I designed the home with a backbone following the curve of the site, and all rooms are an extension of that. There are three main structures, two connecting spaces, and two front entrances.

FACING PAGE: A pool cabana offers the family a shaded conversation spot in the summer. There are also four submerged seats next to the cabana for relaxing.
Photographs by Peter Rymwid Photography

Sussan Lari Architect PC

While some designers think outside of the box, others completely toss the box aside—that is Sussan Lari. With an insatiable urge to create, Sussan started her namesake firm after branching out from a role in a corporate architecture setting. She wanted something more, something better, and began working with a close-knit team in Roslyn, New York.

As times change, so do the needs of a family and the function of the home. The team at Sussan Lari Architect recognizes that and designs homes that make sense for today's lifestyle and fit a family's daily activities. Because of her ultra-creative approach, Sussan seeks out homeowners with open minds—the fewer rules they have, the better. She has reinvented the concept of the traditional layout, so it's best to toss aside standard notions of grand foyers and oversized spaces. Her creativity is most beneficial to a family that doesn't demand the norm.

Sussan starts every project at zero—no formulas, no preconceptions. From there, she maintains a close relationship with the client and has her hand in evert step of the process. Where some architects shy away from getting their hands dirty, Sussan jumps right in. She works on a home at every stage, including the construction process, interior design, and landscaping.

BELOW: The pool functions as a three-in-one space. It has a lap pool, water volleyball area, and a lounge.

FACING PAGE TOP: With a seamless stone floor, the pool cabana looks opens up toward the house and reveals the strong indoor-outdoor connection that appears throughout the home's design.

FACING PAGE BOTTOM: When the homeowner shared their story of winning an artistically designed paddle board by Nicole Miller, I incorporated the vibrant piece into the backyard. It adds a fun, bright, personal touch to the outdoor shower.
Photographs by Peter Rymwid Photography

"Spaces impact people's well-being. That's why design is so important."
—Sussan Lari

ABOVE LEFT: The floating staircase serves as the spine of the house, connecting all three levels. It is surrounded by a stone wall that extends the full height of the house and three-story window wall.

ABOVE RIGHT: A connecting passage sits above the mudroom and has views of the garden below.

RIGHT: I wanted the tea room to have plenty of natural light, so the large windows allow the often-used space to fill up with sunshine.

FACING PAGE: From the rear of the home, the connecting points of the home are clear. They link the home from outside in, and from front to back. They encourage the effortless flow of the movement within the layout. We used slate with accent copper for the roofs.
Photographs by Peter Rymwid Photography

BELOW: We used all-natural materials on this home. I was fully involved with all aspects of the design, including furniture and finishes. Natural stone, wood, and glass were used and I purposely stayed away from any synthetic or unhealthy materials.

FACING PAGE: The homeowner wanted the dining space to have a comfortable feel—like a piano bar. I softened the room with upholstered chairs and avoided heavy, bulky furniture.
Photographs by Peter Rymwid Photography

"Part of my job as an architect is to educate people, to help them understand why design matters."
—Sussan Lari

"*I constantly try to reinvent myself. I don't want to repeat the same design.*"
—Sussan Lari

BELOW: Kitchens are a common gathering place in any home, so I wanted to keep that space open and accessible. The flow of the kitchen to the breakfast room—and extending spaces—allows the area to accommodate large groups without feeling tight. It's a comfortable, smart layout.

FACING PAGE: Behind the bar is a stone slab, which ties to the kitchen, where the same stone is used on the island. The bar gives the dining room a festive, fun element and furthers the homeowner's wish to have a jazz-lounge feel.
Photographs by Peter Rymwid Photography

Thierry Pfister Architecture & Design

Thierry Pfister Architecture & Design creates homes with two simple key elements in mind: light and space. Swiss-born founding principal Thierry Pfister knows that true luxury is not found in adornment or excess, but rather in the complex relationship of light and space, and the way these essential elements play together to create the unique feel and soothing atmosphere of a home.

This singular approach enables Thierry and his firm to craft exceptional houses while drawing from two main sources of inspiration: the homeowner and the site environment. All designs start with a deep understanding of the client's lifestyle, dreams, and desires. After all, a home is so much more than a set—it's a determining factor, unique to each client, in enhancing the quality of life. The site personality and the surrounding aesthetic, be it natural or urban, is the other essential factor. A house must not only complement and effortlessly blend in with its environment; it should also create a nurturing bond between the occupant and their surrounding environment.

Based in New York City and the Hamptons, Thierry and his firm bring more than 20 years of experience to every project. They understand that the best design does not come from a predominant aesthetic but rather reveals itself through a process of discovery. Thierry therefore encourages every homeowner to remain true, honest, and open during the design of the home and to remember that architecture is a process. It's a journey that clients take with the architect in order to create a home that reflects their depth and their soul. It is that trust and mutual involvement that will guarantee the most beautiful, complex, vibrant, and fulfilling home.

BELOW & FACING PAGE: The home is meant to honor the sweeping natural views and the client's quest for serenity. This begins with the outdoor living spaces. The property sits in a landscape primarily made of sand, pine trees, and beach grasses. Shallow steps and multi-level decks connect the garden, swimming pool, and entertainment areas and effortlessly elevate you from the natural grade to the house's main level. While the sculptural pool cabana frames the calm waters of Gardiner's Bay, multiple roof overhangs provide the perfect indoor-outdoor lifestyle and further blur the boundaries between the home and nature.
Photographs by John Musnicki, Graphic Image Group

BELOW & FACING PAGE: The homeowner is an avid art collector, so we designed a white, understated interior so as not to take anything away from the artwork. This elegant, neutral look also complemented the midcentury modern furniture throughout the house. Originally the home had a formal, compartmented layout, but we reconfigured the plan to let the spaces flow and give an airy feel to the interior. The traditional French doors were replaced with oversized, glass sliding doors to reveal the long, stunning views from anywhere in the house. White cabinetry and rich brown Ipe decking was used as a nod to the yachts that can be seen on the water. The raked-limestone lining in the powder room and fireplace mantel echo the sand ripples of the surrounding dunes and beaches.
Photographs by John Musnicki, Graphic Image Group

"A house is not about what you want to be, it's about who you are in a deeper and truer way. Architecture is about your life in that home."
—Thierry Pfister

BELOW & FACING PAGE: Located only 15 minutes from downtown Washington, DC, this home puts its focus on the nearby Potomac River and surrounding forest. Ideally, you'd forget the house is even there, or have difficulty determining whether you're outside or in. We relied on "dry" architecture—sustainable materials like glass, steel, and brushed aluminum—for the exterior, while the interior features warm woods such as fine-grain maple plywood. With the roof elegantly sloping to the ground, it feels like you're in the clouds.
Photographs by Ken Wyner

Travis Price Architects

When approaching a project, Travis Price Architects keeps a trio of tenets in mind: ecology, mythology, and technology. By blending all three, the firm—led by environmental pioneer, author, educator, and philosopher Travis Price—can create buildings that don't just satisfy the needs of today, but endure and innovate well into the future. Focusing on the humanity of each structure and using the homeowner's unique story and needs as a guideline in concert with the specifics of the site, Travis Price Architects ensures that all its creations possess a true spirit of place.

In addition to striking and eco-friendly residences, the firm has designed AIA award-winning commercial and institutional buildings in the U.S., Asia, Europe, and the Americas. Price is responsible for the world's largest solar building and installed the first wind machine in Manhattan as well as coined the term "passive solar" with his early green architectural works in New Mexico. Since 1975, he has won a litany of design awards, including the coveted Fellow of the American Institute of Architecture Title for his unique contributions to the field of architecture. Today he is based in Washington, DC, but designs, consults, and lectures throughout the country and abroad.

BELOW: Beams of light guide guests to the home's entrance, flanked by copper walls that were given their patina onsite with an eco-friendly chemical. A glass railing shields a drop of 20 feet, then another of 350 feet, down to the river.

FACING PAGE TOP: The warm expanse of the living room is enhanced by a minimalist aesthetic—minimalist, but not sterile. A copper fireplace echoes the material used outside.

FACING PAGE CENTER: The same tile used outside is carried through into the home, providing a sense of continuity. It also allows for the easy transfer of potted plants from indoors to out throughout the seasons. The reflective quality of the roof bounces light into the living spaces, lessening the need for artificial illumination.

FACING PAGE BOTTOM: A set of broad stairs cascades down to the media room and children's bedrooms, granting extra privacy for the ground-floor master suite.
Photographs by Ken Wyner

ABOVE LEFT: We were able to save most of the trees on the site that otherwise would have been torn down by a standard building. The surveyor actually measured incorrectly, so we compensated by cutting two feet into the house so that one tree could survive.

ABOVE RIGHT: Though there are neighbors nearby on both sides, I wanted my home to feel like it's all alone in the forest. But in reality, you can be at the White House in only 20 minutes.

LEFT: The entire house is hanging by red steel cables that go 35 feet into the ground. It's like a suspension bridge, floating with the aid of 60-foot steel columns and rock-filled cannisters that prevent the house from moving in strong weather. The translucent walls allow light in, but anyone outside can't see in.

FACING PAGE: The ground floor of my home is like one big loft—even the 360-degree fireplace is open. The aqua spiral staircase spans all four floors and also facilitates return air flow.
Photographs by Ken Wyner

"Every time you encounter a technical problem, it's an opportunity to make a cool aesthetic decision."
—Travis Price

"Architecture is about the story and the idea, not just the ecology and the building."
—Travis Price

ABOVE LEFT: Surrounded by historic colonials, this Washington D.C. home stands out like a shimmering, misty mirage. After stripping the structure down to just brick and glass, we wrapped the exterior in perforated stainless steel to get this effect.

ABOVE RIGHT: The teal spiral staircase leads up to the roof deck, which has amazing, 360-degree views of three major Washington, D.C. churches. At night, the twinkling lights are just spectacular.

RIGHT: The pivoting front door is speckled with divots, some of which are eyeholes placed at different levels so that kids and pets can also look out.

FACING PAGE LEFT: Bump-outs in the kitchen and guest room mean you can look not just out of the windows, but also below and above. After 25 years of living in a traditional home, the owners decided it was time to do something modern and fun.

FACING PAGE BOTTOM: Each of the four floors has a glass bridge running front to back, and a translucent stairwell hung by steel cables is encased in glass, acoustically separating it from the living areas.
Photographs by Ken Wyner

ABOVE: This West Virginia home is located near both a river and set of trees that fork together, so that idea inspired the layout. The guest suite is completely separate from the rest of the home, on its own end of the building.

LEFT: We were able to save all the trees, even the ones growing into the house, and the effect is almost like you're camping.

FACING PAGE TOP: The entire home is floating off the ground, with two curved roofs that feed rainwater into the trees and a little dipping pool in the back.

FACING PAGE BOTTOM: We had to think about the trees' sub-roots, so we carefully placed columns around each one so that none got damaged and then installed a sprinkling system underneath the house. The end result is indoor-outdoor trees that are super-healthy and truly bring the outdoors in.
Photographs by Ken Wyner

Trout Design Studio

Michael Lee Beidler has always been interested with the intimate connection between sentient beings and their contextual environments. As a child, he would watch and learn from people, animals, and other living creatures as they interacted with each other and the world around them, whether that was people in their homes, deer playing in a field, or carpenter ants foraging in the rain forest. The interconnected nature of all living things and the way we craft our living environments for comfort, pleasure, worship, or to protect and nurture ourselves has always fascinated Beidler, and led him to found his own full-service architectural and interior design atelier.

The Trout Design Studio team always strives to make their projects as real, honest, exciting, and full of wonder and discovery as possible. To do that, they watch and listen intently to what their clients are—and aren't— saying about their needs and wants, and also the project's context. For Beidler, the solution to any question or problem lies within its context, and it's finding the correct solution among many that results in a project that not only satisfies the "now" but also the "future."

BELOW TOP: Utilizing the material pallet of the main modern shed-style home, we created a new garage and guest house.

BELOW BOTTOM: The new living room and gallery hall lead to the master suite, visually terminating at the legacy oak tree outside.

FACING PAGE: Everything in this Warrenton, Virginia, home was designed to be the highest efficiency and lowest maintenance possible, with a whole-house geothermal heating and cooling system and full solar array allowing the property to function 100-percent "off the grid." The ying-yang axis of this farm guest house project is the fire pit in the south and hot tub to the north. The finished palette of the steel-framed wall of doors, brass-screened and mahogany porch, and raw CMU block wall materials all reflect the vernacular materials of the existing farm buildings of the site. A new swimming pond was created out across the 10-acre front yard. *Photographs by Max Sall Photography*

"A room's most important element is its relationship to context, scale, and light."
—Michael Lee Beidler

BELOW & FACING PAGE: Heated wide-board birch floors complement the layering of fireplaces from indoors to the outdoor summer porch beyond. The home's entry point has views of the sunrise, expansive lawn, new swimming pond, and pastural Virginia countryside. Photographs by Max Sall Photography

"Inspiration comes from the context of each project as it touches the world looking inward and outward."
—Michael Lee Beidler

BELOW: We designed this property for a family who was originally from Santa Monica. They wanted to integrate a California influence into their New Jersey home, rather than the more traditional housing stock of Tudor and colonial styles that dominate many of the local neighborhoods. The front façade relies on stucco and aluminum along with the warmth of wood grain to provide a sleek, modern approach.

FACING PAGE: The blending of the interior and exterior was important to the family and reflected how they live, so we integrated a range of outdoor, transitional areas, including the second-floor balcony off the master suite and a patio at the first level. The homeowner happens to be a mixed media artist and he designed the mural that's painted on the stucco by the patio; it brings energy and a punch of color to this gathering area.
Photographs by Amanda Kirkpatrick

Z + Architects

If asked about his firm's style, Michael Scro, a principal of Z+ Architects, would say that it is unlimited — unlimited by any style or specific aesthetic, that is. Rather, he and his team are most excited by listening to the needs of their clients and then applying their creativity to develop diverse design solutions that fit the logistical framework, context, and budget of each project. So, it is perhaps no surprise that the team finds inspiration in many places—from art, to music, food, travel, and other architecture and design disciplines.

The principles that guide Z+ Architects' design approach across all projects include the universal importance of natural light, durable materials, and careful attention to how a building relates to its exterior site. In tandem with sister company, Z+ Interiors, the firm offers a seamless and collaborative design experience that's highly inspired. With an eye towards enduring character, details, and livability, they've designed award-winning homes, offices, restaurants, and special needs buildings throughout New Jersey as well as the Hamptons, Connecticut, Pennsylvania, and Vermont.

Trust and long-term relationships with all of their clients, as well as the builders who help turn visions into reality, is likewise paramount with the team at Z+ Architects. They strive to make their clients' role as simple and enjoyable as possible with meaningful and clear ideas and solutions while using their extensive expertise and experience to offer guidance at every step of the way.

BELOW: We prioritized natural light in the design with large-scale windows—especially across the more private rear elevation of the house. The extensive use of glass also further helped unite the indoors and the outdoors, inviting view and light into the principal living spaces.
Photograph by Amanda Kirkpatrick

First Floor Plan

Second Floor Plan

BELOW TOP: The light-filled, master suite opens onto its own private balcony that overlooks the pool and patio below. Our interior design firm, Z+ Interiors, ensured that the clean, modern aesthetic of the home's architecture was likewise celebrated on the inside while utilizing elements such as plants, warm woods, and bright, fresh hues to resonate with the natural beauty outside.

BELOW BOTTOM LEFT: The light fixture in the foyer casts amazing shadows throughout the day and night to enliven the entry space. Its sculptural form, comprised of black lines, reinforces similar themes at the interior and exterior of the home.

BELOW BOTTOM RIGHT: The line drawing echoes the traced character of the chair for an impactful, unifying effect. We also brought in a subtle California vibe with a palm tree, again echoing the family's West Coast roots.
Photographs by Amanda Kirkpatrick

BELOW TOP: We opted to not orient the main staircase in the traditional fashion in the entry foyer, instead hiding it from sight and making it more functionally convenient for the family. The intriguing effect of the mahogany slats across the flat wall offers a sense of movement while both warming the space and bringing in light to the stairwell.

BELOW BOTTOM: The open floor plan accommodates the kitchen, dining area, and living room in one large, interrelated space that dynamically opens out to the patio and pool through the wall of glass. We customized the walnut dining table to precisely fit the space; the walnut bar countertop in the kitchen cohesively unites these two zones.
Photographs by Amanda Kirkpatrick

BELOW TOP: By eliminating upper cabinets, we were able to maintain a streamlined kitchen design where lower cabinets and an island as well as a walk-in pantry create plenty of storage space, without visually cluttering the wall with cabinetry. Intentionally mismatched elements—like the light feature above the dining table and the singular yellow bar stool — turn into unexpected, lyrical details that offer visual impact and personality.

BELOW BOTTOM: We commissioned the resin shower panel from an artist to reflect a soothing, spa-like form in the all-white guest bathroom on the first floor. That this cool accent piece also has a certain sea-like quality is kismet, given the family's former oceanside life in Santa Monica.
Photographs by Amanda Kirkpatrick

"Seamlessly integrating the exterior architecture design with the interior aesthetic is nothing short of a necessary luxury that achieves a unified, elegant, and elevated result."
—Michael Scro

We are proud to present...

Our Finest Modern Architects

WESTERN US

Aidlin Darling Design
500 Third Street
San Francisco, CA 94107
415.974.5603

Allied8 Architecture
1221 W Pike street
Seattle, WA 98102
206.324.2420

Appleton Partners
1556 17th Street
Santa Monica, Ca 90404
310.828.0430

ArchitecTor 17
2930 E Northern Avenue
Suite 100
Phoenix, AZ 85028
602.750.8800
architector.com

Architectural Workshop 25
2 Kalamath Street
Denver, CO 80223
303.788.1717
archshop.com

Architecture Studio 35
316 Sycamore Ave
Mill Valley, CA 94941
415.381.3536
architecturestudioonline.com

Atelier AM
7956 West 3rd Street
Los Angeles, CA 90048
323.951.0500

Brewster McLeod Architects 41
112 South Mill Street
Unit B, Top Floor
Aspen, CO 81611
970.544.0130
brewstermcleod.com

Candeleria Design
23301 W. 40th Street
Scottsdale, CA 85016
602.258.2211

David Vandervort Architects
2000 Fairview Ave
Seattle, WA 98102
206.784.1614

Dean Larkin Design 45
7494 Santa Monica Bl, Ste 303
West Hollywood, CA 90046
323.654.7500
deanlarkindesign.com

Deforest Architects
1148 NW Leary Way
Seattle, WA 98107
206.262.0820

Demetriou Architects 55
Vassos Demetriou
5555 Lakeview Drive Suite 200
Kirkland, WA 98033
425.827.1700
demetriouarchitects.com

Don Young & Associates
1435 Northwest 19th Avenue
Portland, Oregon 97209
503.292.2107

Donald Joseph Inc 67
2620 21st Street
Sacramento, CA 95818
916.456.2300
donaldjoseph.com

DTF Design
Dana Foster
Seattle, WA 98211
425.444.3038

EYRC Architects
10865 Washington Blvd
Culver City, CA 90232
310.838.9700
eyrc.com

(fer) Studio 71
1159 E Hyde Park Blvd.
Inglewood, CA 90302
310.672.4749
ferstudio.com

Gelotte Hommas Architecture
3025 112th Avenue NE
Bellevue, WA 98004
425.828.3081

Georgis & Mirgorodsky
La Jolla, CA 92016
212.288.6280
gma.nyc

Giulietti / Schouten Architects
2800 NW Thurman St.
Portland, Oregon 97210
503.223.0325
gsarchitects.net

Higgins Architects
3666 N. Miller Rd
Scottsdale, AZ 85251
480.990.8897
higginsarch.com

Hoogland Architecture
6280 S Valley View Bl
Las Vegas, NV 89118
702.343.1850

Hoopes & Associates 77
333 Montezuma Ave, Suite 200
Santa Fe, NM
505.986.1010
hoopesarchitects.com

Ike Kligerman Barkley Architects
San Francisco, CA 94103
415.371.1850
ikekligermanbarkley.com

Intermind Design
609 Lidster Place
New Westminster, BC V3L 5E2
604.338.9936

INTERSTICE Architects 85
1173 Sutter Street
San Francisco, CA 94109
415.285.3960
intersticearchitects.com

Intrinsik Architecture 95
111 North Tracy Avenue
Bozeman, Montana 59715
406.582.8988
intrinsikarchitecture.com

James Hann Design, AIA
9834 E Kalil Dr
Scottsdale, AZ 85260
480-661-0517

JDL Development, Inc
2314 NW Savier Street
Portland, OR 97210
503.248.2030

Jones Studio
205 S Wilson Street
Tempe, AZ 85281
602.264.2941

KHA Architects   103
72-185 Painters Path, Suite A
Palm Desert, CA 92260
760.776.4068
kristihanson.com

Kendel Design Collaborative
6115 Cattletrack Road
Scottsdale, AZ 85281
480.951.8558

Landry Design Group
1818 Sepulveda Bl
Los Angeles, CA 90025
310.444.1404

M•Designs Architects   113
4121 El Camino Real, Ste 200
Palo Alto, CA 94306
605.565.9036
mdesignsarchitects.com

M-A Architects
2329 W Main Street, Ste. 301
Littleton, CO
303.730.7300

Maria Ogrydziak Architecture   121
241 B Street
Davis, CA 95616
530.400.5030
oarch.com

McClean Design
190 S. Glassell St
Orange, CA 92886
714.505.0556

Mark English Architects   131
523 San Francisco Street
San Francisco, CA 94133
415.391.0186
markenglisharchitects.com

Mark Stewart Home Design   135
22582 SW Main Street
Suite 309
Sherwood, OR 97140
503.701.4888
markstewart.com

Nest Architecture
4248 Overland Avenue
Culver City, CA 90230
310.559.9900

Norm Applebaum Architect   145
9830 Edgelake Drive
La Mesa, CA 91941
619.463.1867
normapplebaum.com

Peter Vincent Architects
1021 Smith Street Penthouse
Honolulu, HI 96817
808.524.8255

PIQUE Collaborative Architects
1135 NW 15th Street
Bend, OR 97703
541.382.2001

OpenSpace Architecture   155
165 1st Street E.
North Vancouver, BC, V7L 1B2
1.604.984.7722
openspacearchitecture.com

Pinnacle Archectural Studio
9484 W Flamingo Rd
Las Vegas, NV 89147
702.940.6920

POETZL architecture & design
5070 N 40th Street
Phoenix, AZ 85018
480.338.1632

Prentis Balance Wickline
Seattle, WA 98102
206.283.9930

Reid Smith Architects   167
212 S Tracy Avenue
Bozeman, MT 59715
406.587.2597
reidsmitharchitects.com

Richard Meier & Partners
1001 Gayley Avenue
Los Angeles, CA 90024
310.208.6464

Richard Luke Architects   175
9061 W Sahara Ave Suite 105
Las Vegas, NV 89117
702.838.8468
richardlukearchitects.com

Robb Studio, Inc.
5877 S Louthan St,
Littleton, CO
303.908.4430

Semple Brown
1160 Santa Fe Drive
Denver, CO
303.571.4137

Shed Architects
1401 S Jackson
Seattle, WA 98144
206.320.8700

Shelterwerk
1904 Franklin St.,Ste 310
Oakland, CA 94612
510.595.3836

Sinclair Building Architecture Design   183
PO Box 8114
Aspen, CO 81612
970.925.4269
sin-bad.com

Spry Architecture
2730 W Agua Fria Frwy
Phoenix, AZ 85027
602.795.5886

Steelhead Architecture   191
201 SE 3rd Avenue
Portland, OR 97214
503.348.8874
steelheadarchitecture.com

Sutton Suzuki Architects
39 Forest Street
Mill Valley, CA 94941
415.383.3139

Tierney Conner Architecture
363 17th Street
Oakland, CA 94612
510.531.0540

Will Bruder Architects
4200 N Central Avenue
Phoenix, AZ 85012
602.312.7339

Yellowstone Architects
312 Accola Drive
Bozeman, MT 59715
406.579.8450

"Great architecture is born from the single mind focused on a timeless concept."
—Norm Applebaum, AIA

We are proud to present...
Our Finest Modern Architects

CENTRAL US

42° North - Architecture + Design   197
6744 Cascade Road SE
Grand Rapids, MI 49546
616.340.8047
42northarchitects.com

2 R/Z
1629 N Elston
Chicago, Illinois 60642
773.384.4400

A Parallel Architecture   205
803 1/2 West Avenue
Austin, Texas 78701
512.464.1199
aparallel.com

AHS Design Group   209
512.577.3644
ahsdesigngroup.com

AMR Architects, Inc.
100 River Market Avenue, Suite 301
Little Rock, AR 72201
501.375.0378

ALTUS Architecture + Design   215
420 Second Street
Excelsior, MN 55331
612.333.8095
altusarch.com

Andersson / Wise
807 Brazos Street, Suite 800
Austin, TX 78701
512.476.5780

Angelini & Associates Architects   223
113 East Ann Street
Ann Arbor, MI 48104
734.998.0735
angeliniarchitects.com

Surber Barber Choate + Hertlein Architects
675 Ponce De Leon Ave
Atlanta, GA 30308
404.872.8400

Barley Pfeiffer Architecture
1800 W. Sixth Street
Austin, TX 78703
512 476-8580

Bruns Architecture   229
207 E Buffalo Street, Suite 315
Milwaukee, WI 53202
414.763.0010
brunsarchitecture.com

Collaborative DesignWorks
4415 Woodhead St
Houston, TX 77098
713.826.2380

Core 10 Residebtial
4501 Lindell Bl
St Louis, MO 63108
314.726.4858

deMX Architecture
104 N East Ave
Fayetteville, AR 72701
479.966.4871

Destree Design Architects, Inc   235
222 W Washington Ave., #310
Madison, WI 53703
608.268.1499
destreearchitects.com

Element 5 Architecture
1212 Chicon St. Suite 101
Austin, TX 78702
(512) 473-8228

Fazio Architects
308-B Congress Ave.
Austin, TX 78701
512.494.0643

Fennell Purifoy Architects
100 River Bluff Dr # 320
Little Rock, AR 72202
501.372.6734

Genesis Architecture LLC   241
Kenneth Dahlin
1055 Prairie Drive, Suite D
Racine, WI 53406
262.752.1894
genesisarchitecture.com

Goldberg Design Group   245
40 1st Street NW
Carmel, IN 46032
317.582.1430
goldbergdesigngroup.com

Hollenbeck Architects
3701 Kirby Drive, Suite 912
Houston, TX 77098
713.529.5535

HUFFT
3612 Karnes Boulevard
Kansas City, MO 64111
816.531.0200

JBLD LLC
243 N. Fifth St. Suite 200
Columbus, OH 43215
614.228.7311

CCWIV Architecture
3420 Constance Street
New Orleans, LA 70115
504.669.5057

John Grable Architects   249
John Grable, FAIA
222 Austin Highway #1
San Antonio, TX 78209
210.820.3332
johngrable.com

KEM Studio
1515 Genessee ST, Suite 11
Kansas City, MO 64102
816.756.1808

Malone Maxwell Borson Architects   259
718 N Buckner Bl, Suite 400
Dallas, Texas 75218
214.969.5440
mmbarchitects.com

Mathison | Mathison Architects   267
560 5th Street NW #405
Grand Rapids, MI 49504
616.920.0545
mathisonarchitects.com

Morgante-Wilson Architects   273
2834 Central Street
Evanston, IL 60201
847.332.1001
morgantewilson.com

Murphy Mears Architects, Inc.
1973 West Gray, Suite 13
Houston, TX 77019
713.529.9933

Norman D. Ward Architect
240 Loma Blanca Lane
Cresson, TX 76035
817.946.4472

Peter Vincent Architects
327 E 4th Street
Waterloo, IA 50703
808.524.8255

Silo AR + D
Cleveland, OH
Fayette, AR
330.354.1383

Snow Kreilich Architects 281
219 N Second Street, Ste 120
Minneapolis, MN 55401
612.359.9430
snowkreilich.com

Stern and Bucek Architects
1610 Commerce Street
Houston, TX 77002
713.527.0186

Steven Ginn Architects 285
6173 Center Street
Omaha, NE 68106
402.991.1599
stevenginn.com

Studio 8 Architects
611 W 15th Street
Austin, TX 78701
512.473.8989

Tabberson Architects 291
1937 W Royale Drive
Muncie, IN 47304
317.371.3692
tabbersonarchitects.com

Welch Hall Architects
820 Exhibition Avenue Suite 4
Dallas, TX 75226
214.327.3707

SOUTHEASTERN US

ACM Design Architecture
103 Underwood Road, Suite F
Fletcher, NC 28732
828.684.9884

Architectural Collaborative 297
1328 Prince Avenue, 2nd Floor
Athens, GA 30606
706.355.3010
arcollab.net

Arcspace Studio
304 Franklin Street
Huntsville, AL 35801
256.536.1160

BarberMcMurry Architects
505 Market Street, Suite 300
Knoxville, TN 37902-2175
865.934.1915

Borrero Architecture 301
160 SW 12th Ave, Suite 101-C
Deerfield Beach, FL, 33442
561.271.01.64
borreroarch.com

BILD Design Constructs
7721 Leake Avenue
New Orleans, LA 70118
504.861.0042

Brown Davis Architecture & Interiors 307
901 Pennsylvania Ave
Suite 3-538
Miami Beach, FL 33139
305.401.7565
browndavis.com

CCWIV Architecture
3420 Constance Street
New Orleans, LA 70115
504.669.5057

Camens Architectural Group 311
3461 Maybank Highway
John's Island, SC 29455
843.768.3800
camensarchitecturalgroup.com

Carlton–Edwards
103 Broadway Street
Asheville, NC 28801
828.274.7554

Content Architecture & Interiors
6 East Bay St #305
Jacksonville, Fl 32202
904.242.6788

DiG Architects
1101 Houston Mill Rd NE
Atlanta, Georgia 30329
404.835.2855

Frederick + Frederick
38 Meridian Road
Beaufort, SC 29907
843.522.8422

Hays + Ewing Design Studio 315
609 E Market St, Suite 203
Charlottesville, VA 22902
434-979-3222
hays-ewing.com

Hughes Umbanhowar Architects
9357 SE Olympus Street
Hobe Sound. FL 33455
772.546-7011

James Knafo Architect, Inc
405 5th Avenue South
Naples, Florida 34102
239.417.1607

Jeffrey Dungan Architect
Mountain Brook, AL 35223
205.322.2057

John M. Holmes Architect
1220 River Road
Birmingham, AL 35244
205.249.4455

Jones Architecture
3239 Henderson Boulevard
Tampa, FL 33609
813.440.5090

Kevan Hoertdoerfer Architects
538 King Street
Charleston, SC 29403
843.724.6002

KZ Architecture 321
3470 E Coast Ave.,Suite H201
Miami, FL 33137
305.865.9911
kzarchitecture.com

Liquid Design
1430 South Mint Street
Charlotte, NC 28203
704.338.9980

LS3P Associates Ltd 325
2 W Washington St., Ste 600
Greenville, SC 29601
864.235.0405
LS3P.com

Mark Macco Architects
472 Osceola Avenue
Jacksonville Beach, FL 32250
904.249.2724

Michael P. Landry
1155 Ward Creek Drive .
Marietta GA 30064
770.425.1465

Paola Leon-Garcia, AIA
8333 NW 53rd Street, suite 105
Doral, FL 33166
305.456.1135

Our Finest Modern Architects

We are proud to present...

SOUTHEASTERN US (continued)

Oxide Architecture
Raleigh, NC 27605
919.832.2207

Pascual Perez Kiliddjian & Associates   333
1300 NW 84th Avenue
Doral, FL 33126
305.592.1363
ppkarch.com

Robert M. Cain Architect
675 Seminole Avenue
Atlanta, GA 30307
404.892.8643

Roger Wade Studio
Kissimmee, FL
407.460.0071

Ross Design Inc
847 Ormewood Terrace SE
Atlanta, GA 30316
404.624.0101

Ryan Thewes Architect
165 Lelawood Circle
Nashville, TN 37209
615.517.4186

Smith and Moore Architects   339
1500 South Olive Avenue
West Palm Beach, FL 33401
561.835.1888
smithmoorearchitects.com

Solstice Planning & Architecture   343
PO Box 25333
Sarasota, FL 34277
941.365.5721
solstice-pa.com

Studio 2LR | Architecture + Interiors
2428 Main Street
Columbia, SC 29201
803.233.6602

Studio9 Architecture   353
315 East Bay St., Ste. 303
Jacksonville, FL 32202
904.353.5967
studio9arch.net

Studio K Architects   359
4800 N Federal Hwy., #104-A
Boca Raton, FL 33431
561.393.2440
skafl.com

Thomas Everett LambDesign & Development
218 S Matanzas Avenue
Tampa, FL 33609
813.879.3358

Trussoni Architecture Group   365
2455 SW 27th Avenue
Miami, FL 33145
305.803.8642
trussoniarchitecture.com

West Architecture Studio
659 Auburn Avenue
Atlanta, GA 30312
404.222.0962

Woody Friese Architecture   373
7844 Grande Shores Drive
Sarasota, FL 34240
954.709.9393
wfriese.com

XMETRICAL
834 Inman Village Parkway NE
Atlanta, GA 30307
404.474.0018

NORTHEASTERN US

Abstract Architecture
313 Broadway
Buffalo, NY 14204
716.812.2596

Allied8 Architecture
1221 W Pike street
Seattle, WA 98102
206.324.2420

ACTWO Architects   383
30 Boston Post Road
Wayland, MA 01778
508.358.1077
actwoarch.com

A. Ginsburg Architects
6608 Route 116
Shelburne, VT
802.989.5436

Always by Design   391
1315 Walnut Street
Suite 320
Philadelphia, PA 19107
215.627.6250
a-x-d.com

Amalgam Studio   395
401 Park Avenue South
Level 10
New York, NY 10016
646.371.2025
amalgam.nyc

Architecture AF
311 N 2nd St
Richmond, VA 23219
804.774.7180

Architecture + Indigo   401
182 Otis Bassett Road
West Tilsbury, MA 02575
508.687.9531
www.architecture-indigo.com

Axiom Architects
Hanover, MA 02339
781.871.2101

Birdseye   407
3104 Huntington Road
Richmond, VT 05477
802.434.2112
birdseyevt.com

BuiltIN Studio
119 W. 23rd Street, Suite 409
New York, NY 10011
212.367.8055

Campaigne Kestner Architects
131 Boston Street
Guilford, CT 06437
203.453.1224

Christian Zapatka Architect 411
1656 33rd Street NW
Washington, D.C. 20007
202.333.2735
christianzapatka.com

Daniel Conlon Architects
11 Grumman Hill Road, Suite 1B
Wilton, CT
203.544.79884

DDA Architects
255 Main Street
Huntington, NY 11743
631.271.5400

Elizabeth Herrmann Architecture + Design
Bristol, VT 05443
802.453.6401

Flavin Architects
175 Portland St #6
Boston, MA 02114
617.227.6717

Foundry Architects
2701 N Charles Street
Baltimore, MD 21218
410.948.3067

Gardner Architects
Silver Spring, MD 20910
301.654.9145

Gertler & Wente Architects 415
145 West 30th Street
11th Floor
New York, NY 10001
212.273.9888
gwarch.com

H C Design
146 Front Street, Suite 211
Scituate, MA 02066
781.545.5700

Hammer Architects 421
19 Bishop Allen Drive
Cambridge, MA 02139
617.876.5121
hammerarchitects.com

Harpole Architects 425
1155 23rd Street NW, # N3C
Washington D.C. 20037
202.338.3838
Jerryharpole.com

HP Rovinelli Architects
Cambridge, MA 02140
617.551.1135

JMKA | architects 431
25 Imperial Avenue
Westport, CT 06880
203.222.1222
jmkarchitects.com

Jacob Lilly Architects
103 Central Street
Wellesley, MA 02482
781.431.6100

Jane Kim Design
New York, NY 10013
212 334 5194

Kaplan Thompson Architects
102 Exchange St
Portland, ME 04101
207 842.2888

KGP design studio 435
Don Paine
1777 Church Street, NW
Washington, DC 20036
202.822.2102
kgpds.com

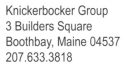

Knickerbocker Group
3 Builders Square
Boothbay, Maine 04537
207.633.3818

KohlMark Group
Burke, VA 22015
703.764.1200

KUBE architecture 439
818 18th Street NW
Suite 600
Washington, D.C. 20006
202.986.0573
kube-arch.com

Lawlor Architects
120 Fourth Street SE
Washington, DC 20003
202.543.4446

Lilian H Weinreich
150 Central Park South #502
New York, NY 10019
917.770.1000

Maryann Thompson Architects 443
741 Mt. Auburn Street
Watertown, MA 02472
617.744.5187
maryannthompson.com

McKay Architects and Design
1182 Broadway, Suite 3B
New York, NY 10001
212.533.4191

McInturff Architects 449
4220 Leeward Place
Bethesda, MD 20816
301.229.3705
mcinturffarchitects.com

McLeod Kredell Architects
3 Frog Hollow Alley
Middlebury, VT 05753
802.989.7242

Meyer & Meyer Architects
396 Commonwealth Avenue
Boston, MA 02215
617.266.0555

Michael Lewis Architects
145 Palisade Street, Suite 307
Dobbs Ferry, NY 10522
914.231.7700

Murdock Solon Architects
New York, NY 10001
212.929.3336

Murdough Design 455
53 Main Street, Suite 203
Concord, MA 01742
978.341.4100
murdoughdesign.com

Muse Architects
7401 Wisconsin Avenue, Suite 500
Bethesda, MD 20814
301.718.8118

Nahra Design Group   461
7059 Blair Road, NW
Suite 104
Washington, DC 20012
202.249.9500
nahradesign.com

Nancy Leary Design
39 Center Street
Brandon, VT
802.558.1444

Ossolinski Architects
1633 Connecticut Avenue NW
Washington, DC 20009
202.966.9449

Overmyer Architects
3213 P Street NW
Washington DC 20007
202.333.5596

Paul Lukez Architecture   465
1310 Broadway, Suite 104
Somerville, MA 02144
617.628.9160
lukez.com

RBL Architects
30 Jacobs Terr.ace
Newton, MA02459
617.527.5300

Richard Williams Architects, PLLC
1909 Q Street NW #200
Washington, DC
202.387.4500

S. Barzin Architect   469
38 Grinnell Street
Jamestown, RI 02835
401.423.7342
sbarzinarchitect.com

Skaala Architecture
58 Bayview Street
Camden ME 04843
774.392.0700

Saniee Architects   475
36 W Putnam Avenue
Greenwich, CT 06830
203.625.9308
sanieearchitects.com

Skaala Architecture
58 Bayview Street
Camden ME 04843
774.392.0700

Slade Architecture
77 Chambers Street
New York, NY
212.677.6380

Stephen Moser Architect
315 West 39th Street, Studio 1608
New York, NY 10018
646.661.5185

Studio 3.0
30 Union Park Street, Suite 506
Boston MA 02118
617.650.2652

Sussan Lari Architect PC   485
1405 Old Northern Bl, Suite 2A
Roslyn, NY 11576
516.625.2916
sussanlari.com

SV Design
126 Dodge Street
Beverly, MA 01915
978.927.3745

Thierry Pfister Architecture & Design   495
150 West 28th Street
Suite 801
New York, NY 10001
646.478.7676
thierrypfister.com

Tokarski + Millemann
1729 Route 35
Wall Township, NJ 07719
732.262.0046

Torchio Architects
205 E. Water Street, Suite A
Centreville, MD 21617
410.758.1000

Travis Price Architects   501
Travis Price, FAIA
1028 33rd Street NW, Suite 320
Washington, DC 20007
202.965.7000
travispricearchitects.com

Trout Design Studio   511
1526 New Hampshire Avenue NW
Washington, DC 20036
202.659.0600
troutdesign.com

Urban Office Architecture
547 West 27th Street, Suite 304
New York, NY 10001
212.233.2290

Wiedemann Architects
5272 River Road, Suite 610
Bethesda, MD 20816
301.652.4022

William L. Feeney Architect
4519 Chesapeake St NW
Washington, DC 20016
202.537.0397

Windigo Architecture & Design
Morristown NJ 07960
973.425.7680

Z + architects   517
240 W Crescent Avenue, Suite D
Allendale, NJ 07401
201.785.8855
zplusarchitects.com

ZeroEnergy Design
156 Milk Street
Boston, MA 02109
617.933.9258

> "Building becomes architecture only when the mind of man consciously takes it and tries with all his resources to make it beautiful, to put concordance, sympathy with nature, and all that into it. Then you have architecture."
>
> —Frank Lloyd Wright

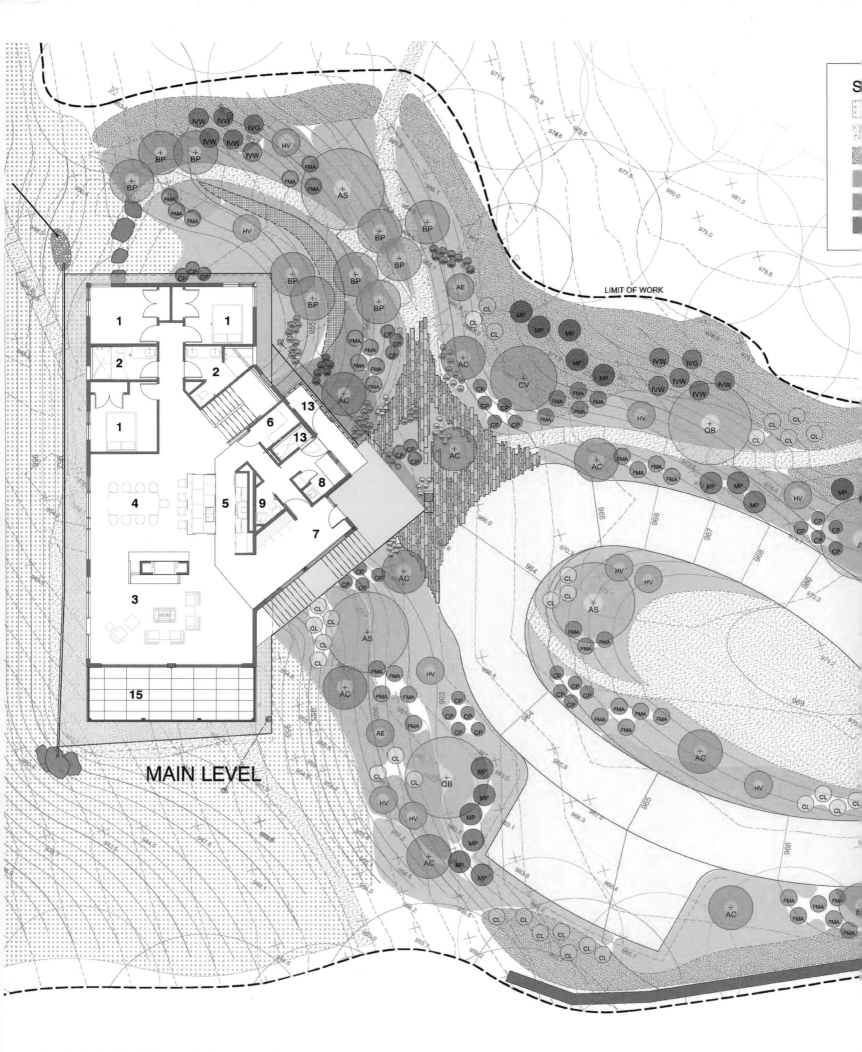

MAIN LEVEL

Site plan by Mathison | Mathison Architects, page 267